中国交通名片丛书

HIGH-SPEED RAILWAY IN CHINA

中国高铁

中国国家铁路集团有限公司　著

人民交通出版社　　中国铁道出版社有限公司

我国自主创新的一个成功范例就是高铁，从无到有，从引进、消化、吸收再创新到自主创新，现在已经领跑世界。要总结经验，继续努力，争取在"十四五"期间有更大发展。

——习近平在京张高铁太子城站考察调研时的讲话
新华社，2021年1月19日

High-speed railway is a successful demonstration of China's independent innovation. China's high-speed railway network has undergone a process from introduction, digestion, absorption and re-innovation to independent innovation, our country is now a world leader in high-speed railway technology. We need to summarize its experience and continue to strive for greater development in the 14th Five-Year Plan period from 2021 to 2025.

Speech by Xi Jinping during his inspection at Taizicheng Station on the Beijing—Zhangjiakou HSR

Xinhua News Agency, January 19, 2021

前言

2021年10月，习近平总书记在联合国第二届全球可持续交通大会开幕式上的主旨讲话中指出，新中国成立以来，几代人逢山开路、遇水架桥，建成了交通大国，正在加快建设交通强国。

今日中国，公路成网，铁路密布，高铁飞驰，巨轮远航，飞机翱翔，邮路畅通，高速铁路、高速公路、城市轨道交通、港口万吨级泊位等规模均跃居世界第一。中国高铁、中国路、中国桥、中国港、中国快递成为亮丽的"中国名片"。

在交通运输波澜壮阔的发展历程中，中国高铁实现了快速发展。截至2023年底，中国高铁营业里程达4.5万公里，占世界高铁总里程的70%以上。中国成为世界上高铁营业里程最长、在建规模最大、商业运营速度最高、高铁技术最全面、运营场景最为丰富的国家。高铁的快速发展，极大地拉近了时空的距离，让出行更加便捷高效，为经济社会发展和国家现代化建设提供了坚实的交通支撑。

我们编写出版《中国高铁》一书，旨在集中勾勒、展现中国高铁发展取得的突出成就，全面呈现中国高铁的创新历程、关键技术、主要特点、功能作用和发展愿景，以帮助大家更好地了解快速发展的中国高铁，并感受中国高铁发展的卓越风采。

中国高铁，从无到有，从追赶到领跑，走过了一条极不平凡的道路。从南到北，从东到西，从沿海到内陆，从高纬度严寒地区到海拔3000米以上的高原地区，中国高铁网络已经覆盖了广泛的地域；从桥梁到隧道，从无砟轨道到大型铁路客站，从列车控制系统到高速列车，从牵引供电到集中调度系统，中国高铁自主创新走在了世界前列……中国高铁每一步都凝聚着无数科技工作者、建设者和管理者的智慧与汗水，每一次跨越都彰显着中华民族自强不息、勇于探索的精神风貌。

奋进新征程，我们要坚持以习近平新时代中国特色社会主义思想为指导，深入学习贯彻习近平总书记关于交通运输的重要论述，继续埋头苦干、担当奉献，再接再厉，再立新功，奋力加快建设交通强国，努力当好中国式现代化的开路先锋，为强国建设、民族复兴作出新的更大贡献。

编者
2024年9月

In October 2021, President Xi Jinping delivered a keynote speech at the opening ceremony of the Second United Nations Global Sustainable Transport Conference, pointing out that since the founding of New China, generation after generation of the Chinese people have worked in the spirit of opening roads through mountains and putting bridges over rivers, and turned China into a country with vast transport infrastructure. Today, Chinese people are redoubling efforts to build China into a country with great transport strength.

China has already built a huge network of highways, railways, ships, airplanes and express delivery routes. China ranks first in the world in terms of the scale of high-speed railways, expressways, urban rail transit, and ports with 10,000-ton berths. China's high-speed railways, roads, bridges, ports and express delivery have become shining "business cards of China".

In the magnificent process of transport development, China's high-speed railway has achieved rapid development. As of the end of 2023, the total operational mileage of China's high-speed railway reached 45,000 kilometers, accounting for more than 70% of the total mileage of high-

PREFACE

speed railway worldwide. China has emerged as the leading nation in high-speed railway, boasting the longest operational mileage, the largest scale of construction projects underway, the highest commercial operation speed, the most comprehensive technology, and the richest array of operational scenarios. The rapid development of high-speed railway has greatly shortened the distance between time and space, made travel more convenient and efficient, and provided solid transportation support for economic and social development and national modernization.

We have compiled and published the book "High-Speed Railway in China" with the aim of comprehensively outlining and displaying the outstanding development achievements of China's high-speed railway. This book comprehensively presents the innovation practices, key technologies, main features and functions, as well as future visions of high-speed railway in China , helping readers gain a deeper understanding of the rapidly developing high-speed railway in China and appreciate its remarkable accomplishments.

China's high-speed railway has traversed an extraordinary journey, started from scratch, and developed from a state of catching up to a position of global leadership. From south to north, from east to west, from coastal regions to inland areas, and from frigid high-latitude regions to plateau regions above 3,000 meters in altitude, China's high-speed railway network has covered an extensive territory. From bridges to tunnels, from ballastless tracks to large railway passenger stations, from train control systems to high-speed trains, from traction power supply to centralized dispatching systems, China's high-speed railway has taken the lead in the world in terms of independent innovation... Every step of China's high-speed railway embodies the wisdom and hard work of countless scientific and technological workers, builders, and managers, and every leap forward demonstrates the unyielding spirit and courage to explore of the Chinese nation.

As we embark on the new journey, we must adhere to the guidance of Xi Jinping Thought on Socialism with Chinese Characteristics for a New Era, thoroughly study and implement the important exposition of General Secretary Xi Jinping on building China's transport strength, continue to work hard, and take on responsibility. We must strive to build China into a country with great transport strength, strive to be the trailblazer in China's modernization drive, and make new and greater contributions to building a powerful country and realizing national rejuvenation.

Editors
September 2024

目　录

001　第 1 章　/　中国高铁概况

007　第 2 章　/　中国高铁创新历程

008　　　蓄势待发
010　　　快速发展
019　　　自立自强

063　第 3 章　/　中国高铁关键技术

064　　　工程建造技术
082　　　高速动车组技术
090　　　列车运行控制技术
092　　　牵引供电技术
096　　　运营管理技术
099　　　风险防控技术

101　第 4 章　/　中国高铁主要特点

103　　　安全可靠
104　　　运力强大
106　　　平稳舒适
107　　　方便快捷

114　　　节能环保
119　　　适用性强

123　第 5 章　/　中国高铁创造美好生活

124　　　极大便利人们出行
126　　　带来"同城效应"
128　　　催生"高铁＋旅游"新业态
130　　　助力区域协调发展
133　　　提供繁荣发展新动能

135　第 6 章　/　中国高铁发展愿景

137　　　更完善
139　　　更高速
147　　　更智能
149　　　更绿色

151　第 7 章　/　中国高铁走向世界

162　后记

CONTENTS

Chapter 1 Overview	**001**
Chapter 2 Innovation Practice	**007**
Know-How Accumulation	008
Fast Development	011
Independent Innovation	020
Chapter 3 Key Technologies	**063**
Engineering Construction	065
High-Speed Train	083
Train Control	091
Traction Power Supply	092
Operational Management	096
Risk Prevention and Control	099
Chapter 4 Main Features	**101**
Safe and Reliable	103
Sufficient and Strong	104
Smooth and Comfortable	106
Fast and Convenient	108
Energy-Saving and Environment-Friendly	114
Applicable and Flexible	119
Chapter 5 HSR for Better Life	**123**
Facilitating Travel	125
Bringing about Urban Cohesion Effect	127
Cultivating New Tourism	129
Contributing to Coordinated Development Across Regions	130
Providing a New Growth Driver	133
Chapter 6 Future Visions	**135**
Wider	137
Faster	139
Smarter	147
Greener	149
Chapter 7 Going Global	**151**
Epilogue	**163**

中国高铁　HIGH-SPEED RAILWAY IN CHINA

　　近年来,按照国家《中长期铁路网规划》和"十一五""十二五""十三五""十四五"规划,中国加快推进高铁建设,"四纵四横"高铁网提前建成运营,"八纵八横"高铁网加密成型。

In recent years, China has accelerated the construction of high-speed railway (HSR) according to the *Medium and Long Term Railway Network Plan* and the eleventh, twelfth, thirteenth and fourteenth Five-Year Plan for National Economic and Social Development of China. The HSR network undergirded by "four north-south and four east-west corridors" had been put into operation ahead of plan and the one by "eight north-south and eight east-west corridors" is being formed at a faster pace.

CHAPTER 第 1 章 | 中国高铁概况

Overview

截至 2023 年底，中国高铁营业里程达 4.5 万公里，占世界高铁总里程的 70% 以上。中国成为世界上高铁营业里程最长、在建规模最大、商业运营速度最高、高铁技术最全面、运营场景最为丰富的国家。

中国高铁技术水平总体迈入世界先进行列，部分领域达到世界领先水平。以智能京张高铁开通运营和时速 350 公里复兴号智能动车组上线运行为标志，中国高铁技术领跑世界。

中国高铁改变了中国人的出行方式。截至 2023 年底，动车组列车累计发送旅客 196 亿人次。目前，高铁承担了中国全社会 23% 左右的旅客发送量、31% 左右的旅客周转量，承担了全国铁路 76% 左右的旅客发送量、66% 左右的旅客周转量，成为中长途旅客运输的主力，基本解决了原来客运高峰期运力严重短缺的问题。

By the end of 2023, China had put into operation 45,000km HSR, accounting for more than 70% of total HSR length in the world, having the largest HSR network both in operation and under construction in the world. With HSR operating at the highest speed under the most various scenarios, China has developed the most complete set of technologies in the world.

As a result, China has been ranked among leading countries in HSR technologies and even led other countries in some fields, such as the intelligent Beijing—Zhangjiakou HSR line and the 350km/h intelligent Fuxing (Rejuvenation) high-speed trains.

China's HSR has changed the way people travel in China. By the end of 2023, the total number of passengers carried by high-speed trains had reached 19.6 billion. Now China's HSR handles about 23% of passenger trips and about 31% turnover of passenger traffic in whole China and about 76% of passenger trips and about 66% turnover of passenger traffic in China's railways. It has become the leading player to transport passengers for medium-distance and long-distance travels, virtually solving the severe capacity shortage issue during traffic rush.

◀ 复兴号智能动车组在长城脚下飞驰
A Fuxing High-Speed Train Gallops at the Foot of the Great Wall

▲ 复兴号动车组跨越京沪高铁南京大胜关长江大桥
A Fuxing High-Speed Train Crosses Nanjing Dashengguan Yangtze River Bridge on Beijing—Shanghai HSR Line

中国高铁　　HIGH-SPEED RAILWAY IN CHINA

---

　　20 世纪 90 年代，中国开始在高铁领域进行创新实践，在较短的时间内取得了重大进步，在高铁技术自主创新上实现重大突破，高铁建设和运营规模迅速跃居世界首位。

China began its research and development on the HSR from the 1990s. With significant progress achieved in short time, China has made major breakthroughs in HSR technology and now ranks first in the world in the scale of the HSR network both in operation and under construction.

第 2 章 中国高铁创新历程

Innovation Practice

■ 蓄势待发

20世纪90年代初到2003年，中国高铁处于技术积累阶段。在此期间，中国开始了发展高铁的探索性研究，对高铁的设计建造、高速列车、运营管理等基础理论和关键技术开展了攻关，为随后高铁的快速发展奠定了坚实基础。

1994年12月22日，全长147公里，由原广州至深圳铁路改建而成的广州至深圳准高速铁路投入运营，最高运营时速达160公里。

1997年至2007年，中国铁路完成六次既有线大提速，繁忙干线提速区段最高运营时速达200公里。

2003年10月12日，全长405公里，新建的秦皇岛至沈阳客运专线（秦沈客专）投入运营，最高运营时速200公里，为高铁建设进行了技术和人才准备。

■ Know-How Accumulation

From the beginning of 1990s to 2003, China had accumulated its knowledge about HSR. During this period, China explored and studied the ways of developing HSR, and solved critical problems in basic theory and key technologies in such fields as HSR design, construction, operation and management, as well as high-speed train manufacture, getting itself ready for fast HSR development later.

▲ 秦沈客专
Qinhuangdao—Shenyang PDL

On December 22, 1994, the 147km Guangzhou—Shenzhen line, a quasi-HSR line with a maximum operating speed of 160km/h upgraded from the existing railway line, was put into operation.

From 1997 to 2007, China had undertaken six major speed-ups for the existing railway lines, increasing the maximum operating speed in the speeded-up sections of busy trunk lines up to 200km/h.

On October 12, 2003, the 405km Qinhuangdao—Shenyang passenger-dedicated line (PDL) with a maximum operating speed of 200km/h, was put into operation, laying a good technology foundation and fostering talents for future HSR construction.

▼ 浙赣铁路（杭州至株洲铁路）是中国第一条按时速200公里标准进行电气化改造的干线铁路，也是全国铁路第六次既有线大提速的标志性工程。

The Zhejiang—Jiangxi railway is the first trunk railway in China to undergo electrification transformation for a speed of 200km/h, and it is also a landmark project for the sixth major speed-ups for the existing railway in China.

■ 快速发展

2004年至2011年，中国铁路以国家顶层规划为契机，大力推动高铁建设，按照"引进先进技术、联合设计生产、打造中国品牌"的指导方针，大力推进高铁技术原始创新、集成创新和引进消化吸收再创新，实现了CRH系列动车组国产化制造，研发了CTCS-2级列控系统，系统掌握了时速250公里和350公里等级高铁整套技术，陆续建成了北京至天津城际铁路（京津城际）、北京至上海高速铁路（京沪高铁）等一批高铁。

▲ 2007年4月18日，时速200公里的CRH2型动车组在上海南站首发。
On April 18, 2007, the CRH2 high-speed train with a speed of 200km/h made its debut at Shanghainan Railway Station.

▲ 京津城际
Beijing—Tianjin Intercity Railway

■ Fast Development

From 2004 to 2011, CHINA RAILWAY had utilized the national planning as an opportunity to promote the HSR construction with great efforts. Guided by the principle of "introducing advanced technology, cooperating with foreign partners in design and production, and building China's own brand", CHINA RAILWAY did its utmost to promote original innovation, integrated innovation and re-innovation after introducing, digesting and absorbing HSR technology, and had realized localized manufacture of CRH high-speed trains, developed CTCS-2 train control system, mastered the complete know-how of 250km/h HSR and 350km/h HSR technology, and built a number of HSR lines including those from Beijing to Tianjin and Shanghai.

中国高铁 | HIGH-SPEED RAILWAY IN CHINA

2004年1月，中国政府发布了《中长期铁路网规划》，提出规划建设"四纵四横"快速客运通道，其中客运专线1.2万公里以上。

2008年8月1日，全长120公里的京津城际开通运营，这是中国第一条设计时速350公里的高铁。

2008年10月，中国政府发布了《中长期铁路网规划（调整）》，提出建设铁路客运专线1.6万公里。

In January 2004, the Chinese Government issued the *Medium and Long Term Railway Network Plan*, proposing to build the "four north-south and four east-west corridors", including over 12,000km passenger-dedicated lines.

On August 1, 2008, the 120km Beijing—Tianjin intercity railway was put into operation. It is the first HSR line with the design speed of 350km/h in China.

In October 2008, the Chinese Government issued a revised version of the *Medium and Long Term Railway Network Plan*, proposing to build 16,000km passenger-dedicated lines.

◀ 北京南站
Beijingnan Railway Station

▽ 天津站
Tianjin Railway Station

2010年2月6日，全长523公里，设计时速350公里，世界上首条修建在大面积湿陷性黄土地区的郑州至西安高速铁路（郑西高铁）开通运营。

On February 6, 2010, the 523km Zhengzhou—Xi'an HSR line with design speed of 350km/h, the world's first HSR line built in large collapsible loess areas, was put into operation.

▼ 西安北站
Xi'anbei Railway Station

▼ 郑西高铁
Zhengzhou—Xi'an HSR Line

▼ 上海虹桥站
Shanghai Hongqiao Railway Station

2011年6月30日，全长1318公里，设计时速350公里，运营列车试验速度最高（时速达486.1公里）的京沪高铁开通运营。

On June 30, 2011, the 1,318km Beijing—Shanghai HSR line, with design speed of 350km/h, was put into operation. On this line, the high-speed train set a speed record of 486.1km/h, the highest test speed of an operation train in the world.

■ 自立自强

自2012年起，中国铁路以实现关键核心技术自主化为目标，加强重点领域技术研发和成果转化，深入开展基础理论研究和重大科技项目攻关，系统掌握了涵盖技术装备、工程建造、运营管理等的高铁核心技术，形成了具有中国特色、全面拥有自主知识产权的高铁成套技术和装备体系，实现了中国高铁安全有序运营、优质服务和一流管理。

近年来，中国高铁向更智能、更安全舒适、更高标准的方向迈进，采用云计算、物联网、北斗定位、人工智能等先进技术，成为世界智能铁路发展的重要引领者，实现了旅客出行更加方便快捷、铁路运营更加安全高效、铁路装备更加绿色环保。

▶ 无砟轨道
Ballastless Track

■ Independent Innovation

In 2012, CHINA RAILWAY began strengthening its research and development (R&D) on technology and the application of the achievements in critical fields, aiming at mastering the know-how of key technologies. It deepened its research on basic theories and worked hard to solve major problems in science and technology. As a result, CHINA RAILWAY has mastered key HSR technologies of equipment, construction and operation and management and developed its own HSR technologies and equipment with Chinese characteristics. All intellectual property rights of these technologies and equipment are owned by CHINA RAILWAY. With all these, CHINA RAILWAY has realized the safe and sound HSR operation, offered quality service for passengers, and showcased its first-class management.

In recent years, China's HSR is becoming more intelligent, more comfortable and safer, aiming at a higher standard. Utilizing advanced technologies of cloud-computing, Internet of Things, Beidou navigation and artificial intelligence, CHINA RAILWAY has become the important leader in developing intelligent railway in the world, offering more convenient and faster travel for passengers, operating HSR lines more safely and efficiently, and making equipment greener and more environment-friendly.

► 冬奥列车驶过北京居庸关长城
High-Speed Train for Beijing 2022 Winter Olympics Passes by the Great Wall of Juyongguan in Beijing

2012年12月1日，全长921公里，设计时速350公里，世界上第一条穿越高寒季节性冻土地区的哈尔滨至大连高速铁路（哈大高铁）开通运营。

On December 1, 2012, the 921km Harbin—Dalian HSR line with design speed of 350km/h, the world's first HSR line crossing the alpine permafrost regions, was put into operation.

▽ 大连北站　　▷ 哈大高铁
Dalianbei Railway Station　　Harbin—Dalian HSR Line

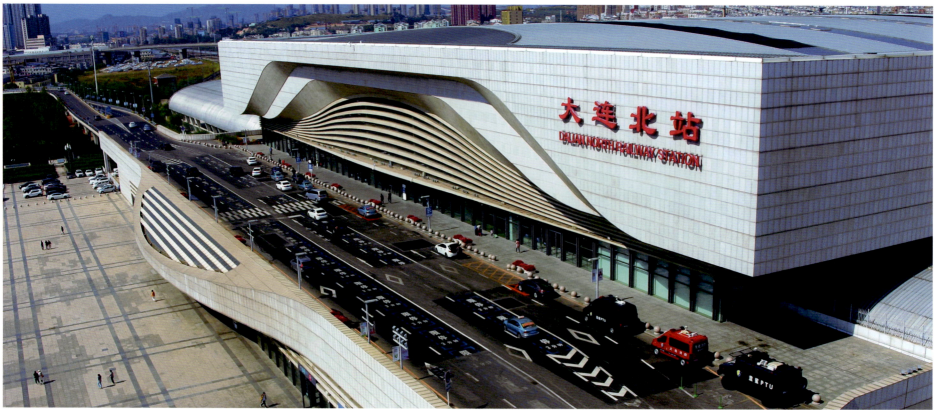

▼ 哈尔滨西站
Harbinxi Railway Station

2012年12月26日，全长2281公里，设计时速350公里，世界上营业里程最长，跨越温带与亚热带、多种地形地质区域和众多水系的北京至广州高速铁路（京广高铁）全线开通运营。

▲ 大连北站
Dalianbei Railway Station

▼ 京广高铁
Beijing—Guangzhou HSR Line

On December 26, 2012, the 2,281km Beijing—Guangzhou HSR line, the world's longest HSR line with design speed of 350km/h, was put into operation. This line travels across temperate zone, subtropical zone, regions with various topographical and geological features and many water systems.

▼ 北京西站
Beijingxi Railway Station

▼ 广州南站
Guangzhounan Railway Station

2013年12月28日，全长1464公里，设计时速250公里至350公里，连接长江三角洲、海峡西岸和珠江三角洲的杭州至宁波至深圳的东南沿海高速铁路（杭深高铁）全线开通运营。

On December 28, 2013, the 1,464km southeast coastal HSR line, with design speed ranging from 250km/h to 350km/h, was put into operation. It extends from Hangzhou to Shenzhen via Ningbo, connecting the Yangtze River Delta to the west side of Taiwan Straits, and then to the Pearl River Delta.

▶ 杭州东站
Hangzhoudong Railway Station

2014年12月26日，全长1776公里，设计时速250公里，世界上一次建成里程最长、穿越戈壁沙漠地带和大风区的兰州至乌鲁木齐高速铁路（兰新高铁）全线开通运营。

On December 26, 2014, the 1,776km Lanzhou—Urumqi HSR line with design speed of 250km/h, the world's longest HSR line built in one phase, was put into operation. This line crosses the Gobi Desert area and windy regions.

▼ 乌鲁木齐站
Urumqi Railway Station

▽ 兰新高铁
Lanzhou—Urumqi HSR Line

2014年12月26日,全长856公里,设计时速300公里,连接西部地区与珠江三角洲的贵阳至广州高速铁路(贵广高铁)开通运营。

▼ 贵广高铁
Guiyang—Guangzhou HSR Line

On December 26, 2014, the 856km Guiyang—Guangzhou HSR line with design speed of 300km/h, connecting the Western region of China to Pearl River Delta, was put into operation.

2015年12月30日，全长653公里，设计时速200公里至250公里，世界上首条穿越热带滨海地区的环岛高铁——海南环岛高速铁路（海南环岛高铁）全线开通运营。

▽ 海南环岛高铁列车飞驰在海岸椰树边
A High-Speed Train Gallops by Coconut Trees on Hainan Island HSR Loop Line

▼ 博鳌站
Boao Railway Station

On December 30, 2015, the 653km Hainan Island HSR loop line with design speed ranging from 200km/h to 250km/h, the world's first line crossing tropical coastal areas, was put into operation.

2016年7月,中国政府发布新的《中长期铁路网规划》,描绘了"八纵八横"高铁网的蓝图,规划到2025年时速250公里及以上高铁营业里程达3.8万公里左右。

2016年7月15日,中国自行设计研制、全面拥有自主知识产权的中国标准动车组,在郑州至徐州高速铁路(郑徐高铁)开展的综合试验中,成功实现时速420公里交会和重联运行。这一试验在世界高铁运营列车历史上尚属首次。

In July 2016, the Chinese Government rolled out the updated *Medium and Long Term Railway Network Plan*, presenting a blueprint of a network undergirded by "eight north-south and eight east-west corridors" and indicating that the HSR lines with speed of 250km/h and above would add up to about 38,000km in 2025.

On July 15, 2016, two Chinese standard high-speed trains developed and manufactured independently with proprietary intellectual property rights, passed by each other in opposite directions on parallel tracks at a speed of 420km/h, both in coupled formation, in a comprehensive test on Zhengzhou—Xuzhou HSR line. This test is the first of its kind carried out with operation trains in the world.

▲ 中国标准动车组在郑徐高铁实现时速 420 公里交会和重联运行
Two Chinese Standard High-Speed Trains Pass by Each Other in Opposite Directions on Parallel Tracks at a Speed of 420km/h Both in Coupled Formation on Zhengzhou—Xuzhou HSR Line

2016年12月28日，全长2252公里，设计时速350公里，中国东西向线路里程最长、经过省份最多的上海至昆明高速铁路（沪昆高铁）全线开通运营。

On December 28, 2016, the 2,252km Shanghai—Kunming HSR line with design speed of 350km/h, the China's longest east-west HSR line crossing most provinces, was put into operation.

▽ 昆明南站
Kunmingnan Railway Station

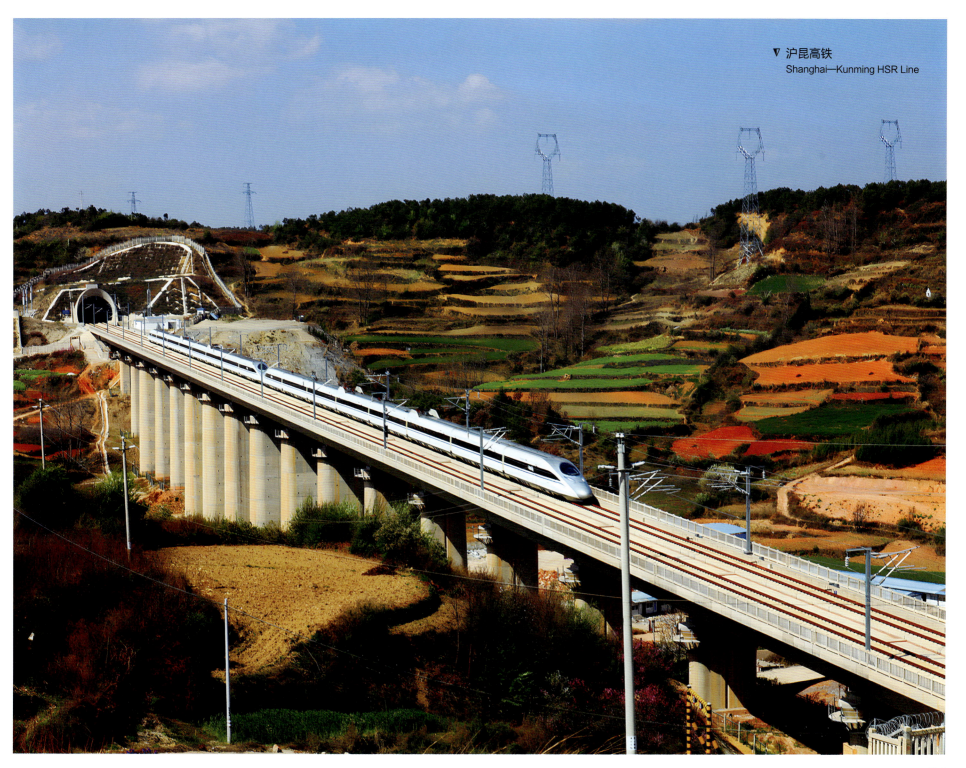

▼ 沪昆高铁
Shanghai—Kunming HSR Line

2017年9月21日，复兴号动车组在京沪高铁常态化按时速350公里高标运营。

On September 21, 2017, Fuxing high-speed trains began to ride on Beijing—Shanghai HSR line at a speed of 350km/h as normal operation.

2017年12月6日，全长658公里，设计时速250公里，中国首条穿越地理和气候南北分界线——秦岭的西安至成都高速铁路（西成高铁）开通运营，破解"蜀道难"取得历史性突破。

On December 6, 2017, the 658km Xi'an—Chengdu HSR line with a design speed of 250km/h, China's first HSR line running through the Qinling Mountains, the geographical and climate boundary between the north and the south of China, was put into operation. It is a historic breakthrough to make Sichuan not difficult for people to access any longer.

▲ 复兴号动车组在京沪高铁实现时速350公里商业运营。
A Fuxing High-Speed Train rides at a speed of 350km/h on Beijing—Shanghai HSR line in commercial operation.

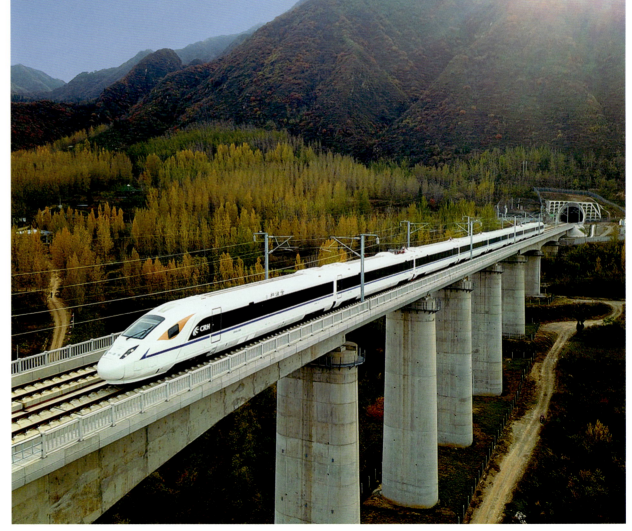

▶ 西成高铁
Xi'an—Chengdu HSR Line

▽ 新场街站
Xinchangjie Railway Station

2018年8月8日，京津城际运行的动车组全部调整为复兴号，常态化按时速350公里高标运营。

On August 8, 2018, high-speed trains on Beijing—Tianjin intercity railway were all changed to Fuxing high-speed trains, which rode at 350km/h as normal operation.

▼ 复兴号动车组飞驰在京津冀大地上
A Fuxing High-Speed Train Speeds on the Land of Beijing, Tianjin and Hebei

▶ 复兴号动车组驶过北京永定门城楼
A Fuxing High-Speed Train Passes by the Yongdingmen Tower in Beijing

2018年9月23日，全长141公里，设计时速200公里至350公里，连接香港和内地的广州至深圳至香港高速铁路（广深港高铁）全线开通运营，香港进入全国高速铁路网。

On September 23, 2018, the 141km Guangzhou—Shenzhen—Hong Kong HSR Line with design speed ranging from 200km/h to 350km/h, connecting Hong Kong to Guangzhou and Shenzhen, was put into operation, incorporating Hong Kong into the national HSR network.

▼ 广深港高铁西九龙站外景
The Exterior of Hong Kong West Kowloon Railway Station on Guangzhou — Shenzhen — Hong Kong HSR Line

▲ 旅客乘坐动感号列车
Passengers in Vibrant Express

▲ 旅客乘广深港高铁抵达香港
Passengers Arrive in Hong Kong by the Guangzhou—Shenzhen—Hong Kong HSR Line

▶ 旅客与动感号列车合影留念
Passengers Take Pictures with Vibrant Express

▼ 少数民族旅客在车厢内欢快舞蹈庆贺成贵高铁开通运营
Passengers from Minority Groups Dance Happily in the Carriage to Celebrate the Opening of Chengdu—Guiyang HSR Line

2019年12月16日，全长648公里，设计时速250公里，穿越乌蒙山区的成都至贵阳高速铁路（成贵高铁）全线开通运营，形成川渝黔地区通往东南沿海地区的快速客运通道。

On December 16, 2019, the 648km Chengdu—Guiyang HSR line with a design speed of 250km/h, crossing Wumeng Mountains, was put into operation, forming an express corridor for passengers from Sichuan, Chongqing and Guizhou to visit the southeast coastal area of China.

▲ 成贵高铁首发列车
High-Speed Train Made its debut on Chengdu—Guiyang HSR Line

2019年12月30日，全长174公里，设计时速350公里，世界上首条智能化高速铁路——北京至张家口高速铁路（京张高铁）开通运营，具有自动驾驶功能的时速350公里复兴号智能动车组同步上线运行，常态化按时速350公里高标运营。从自主设计修建零的突破到世界先进水平，从时速35公里到350公里，京张线见证了中国铁路的发展，也见证了中国综合国力的飞跃。

On December 30, 2019, the 174km Beijing—Zhangjiakou HSR line with a design speed of 350km/h, the first intelligent HSR line in the world, was put into operation. The 350km/h intelligent Fuxing high-speed train equipped with automatic train operation (ATO) device was also unveiled. This line is operated with high standard at the speed of 350km/h in regular mode. The existing Beijing—Zhangjiakou line is the first railway designed and built by Chinese people, while the new Beijing—Zhangjiakou HSR line has led the world in railway technology. From 35km/h to 350km/h, the lines between Beijing and Zhangjiakou have witnessed the development of railway in China and the leap of China's national comprehensive strength.

▲ 京张高铁太子城站
Taizicheng Railway Station on Beijing—Zhangjiakou HSR Line

▼ 京张高铁官厅水库特大桥
Super Major Bridge over Guanting Reservoir on Beijing—Zhangjiakou HSR Line

2020年12月26日，全长617公里，设计时速250公里，中国一次性建成里程最长的有砟高速铁路——银川至西安高速铁路（银西高铁）开通运营。

On December 26, 2020, the 617km Yinchuan—Xi'an HSR line with a design speed of 250km/h, China's longest HSR with ballast track built in one-phase, was put into operation.

▲ 银西高铁开通运营
Yinchuan—Xi'an HSR Line Opens to Traffic

▲ 京雄城际雄安站
Xiong'an Railway Station on Beijing—Xiong'an Intercity Railway

2020年12月27日，全长91公里，设计时速350公里，中国又一条智能化高速铁路——北京至雄安新区城际铁路（京雄城际）开通运营。

On December 27, 2020, the 91km Beijing—Xiong'an intercity railway with a design speed of 350km/h, another intelligent HSR line, was put into operation.

2021年1月22日,全长1198公里,设计时速350公里,东北地区进出关最快速的铁路——北京至哈尔滨高速铁路(京哈高铁)全线开通运营。

▲ 京哈高铁
Beijing-Harbin HSR Line

On January 22, 2021, the 1,198km Beijing—Harbin HSR line with a design speed of 350km/h, the fastest railway channel connecting the northeast of China to the rest of China via Shanhaiguan, was put into operation.

2022年1月6日，以新型复兴号智能动车组为依托，根据北京冬奥会、冬残奥会需求量身打造，搭载5G（第五代移动通信技术）超高清演播室的北京冬奥列车正式在京张高铁上线运行，最高时速达350公里。

On January 6, 2022, the high-speed train for Beijing 2022 Winter Olympics, carrying ultra-high definition studio using 5G telecommunication technology, made its debut on Beijing—Zhangjiakou HSR line, hitting a maximum operating speed of 350km/h. This train was tailored on the basis of new type Fuxing intelligent high-speed train to meet customized requirements of Beijing 2022 Winter Olympics and Paralympics.

▼ 冬奥列车 5G 超高清演播室
Ultra-High Definition Studio Using 5G Telecommunication Technology on High-Speed Train for Beijing 2022 Winter Olympics

▼ 冬奥列车飞驰驶过滑雪小镇
A High-Speed Train for Beijing 2022 Winter Olympics Speeds by Ski Resort

◀ 中国自主研发的世界领先新型复兴号高速综合检测列车创造明线相对交会时速 870 公里世界纪录。

The world-leading Fuxing comprehensive high-speed inspection train independently developed by China made its operation at a relative speed of 870km/h when meeting another train on the open section of a HSR line, creating a new world speed record.

2022 年 4 月 21 日，中国自主研发、世界领先新型复兴号高速综合检测列车，在济南至郑州高速铁路进行的综合试验中，成功实现相对时速 870 公里明线交会运行，创造新的世界纪录。

On April 21, 2022, the world-leading Fuxing comprehensive high-speed inspection train independently developed by China made its operation at a relative speed of 870km/h when meeting another train on the open section of Jinan—Zhengzhou HSR line during a test, setting a new world speed record.

2022年6月20日，复兴号动车组在京广高铁北京西至武汉段常态化按时速350公里高标运营。

On June 20, 2022, Fuxing high-speed trains began to ride on the section of Beijingxi—Wuhan of Beijing—Guangzhou HSR line at a speed of 350km/h as normal operation.

▼ 京广高铁北京西至武汉段时速 350 公里高标运营列车进入武汉站。
High-speed trains operating at a high standard of 350km/h on Section of Beijingxi—Wuhan of Beijing—Guangzhou HSR line pull into Wuhan Railway Station.

2022年6月20日，全长1063公里，设计时速250公里至350公里，中国第一条桥隧比超过90%、穿越复杂险峻山区的郑州至重庆高速铁路（郑渝高铁）全线开通运营。

On June 20, 2022, the 1,063km Zhengzhou—Chongqing HSR line with a design speed ranging from 250km/h to 350km/h, was put into operation. It is the first HSR line that crosses complex and precipitous mountain areas with bridges and tunnels accounting for over 90% of its total length.

▼ 通过神农架站的首列复兴号列车
The First Fuxing High-Speed Train Passing Through Shennongjia Railway Station

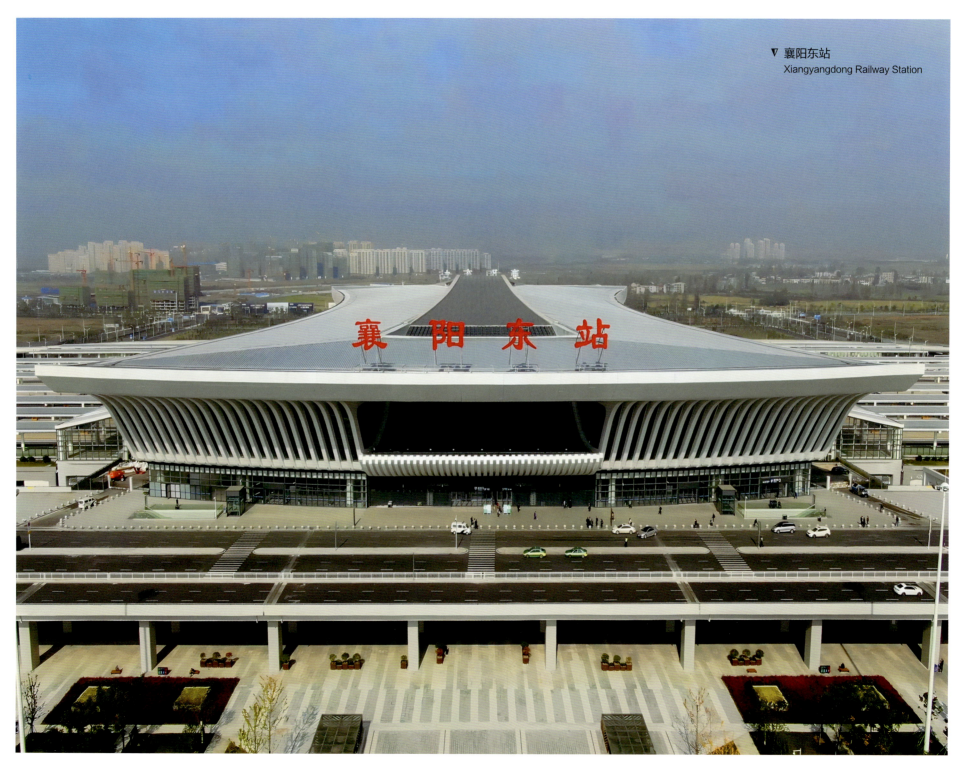

▼ 襄阳东站
Xiangyangdong Railway Station

中国高铁　HIGH-SPEED RAILWAY IN CHINA

　　高铁是中国自主创新的一个成功范例。经过多年的科学研究和工程实践，中国构建了完备的高铁技术体系，覆盖勘察设计、工程建造、高速列车、牵引供电、运营管理、安全保障等各个方面，总体技术水平迈入世界先进行列，部分领域达到世界领先水平，复兴号高速列车迈出从追赶到领跑的关键一步。

HSR is a demonstration of independent innovation in China. With years of R&D and engineering practice, China has developed a complete HSR technology system, covering survey and design, engineering construction, high-speed train, traction power supply, operational management and safety control. Now China's HSR technologies are advanced in the world on the whole and even world-leading in some fields. Fuxing high-speed train is a key step taken by China to shift place from follower to leader in HSR technologies.

第 3 章 中国高铁关键技术

Key Technologies

■ 工程建造技术

中国修建高铁面临的地质条件及气候环境非常复杂，在世界上没有成熟经验可借鉴，完全依靠自主创新形成了独特的工程建造技术优势。近年来，中国建设了一大批适应高寒、高温、干旱、风沙等特殊气候，以及软土、黄土、季节性冻土、岩溶等复杂地质的高铁，具备在各种气候环境和复杂地质条件下建设高铁的能力。

中国拥有世界上最全面的桥梁设计建造技术和现代化的施工装备，先后修建了南京大胜关长江大桥、武汉天兴洲长江大桥、沪苏通长江公铁大桥、平潭海峡公铁大桥、五峰山长江大桥、北盘江铁路大桥等一批跨越大江大河的世界级大跨度高铁桥梁。

中国攻克了城市区大直径盾构隧道、挤压性围岩隧道修建技术难题，建成广深港高铁狮子洋隧道、西成高铁秦岭隧道群、京张高铁新八达岭隧道等10公里以上长大高铁隧道100多座。

中国研发了高铁钢轨、大号码道岔、扣件系统、钢轨伸缩调节器等轨道关键设备，建设了世界上规模最大、技术最先进的无砟轨道系统，无砟轨道正线铺设里程近5.27万公里。

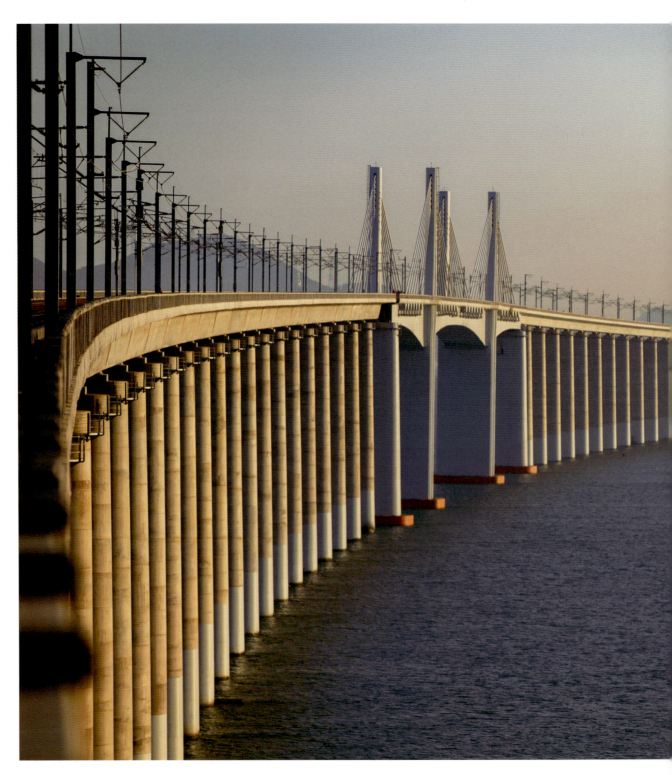

◀ 福厦高铁湄洲湾大桥
Meizhou Bay Cross-Sea Bridge on Fuzhou—Xiamen HSR Line

■ Engineering Construction

China has extremely complicated geological and climatic conditions and there is not much experience for it to draw on from other countries on how to build HSR lines under such circumstances. Through independent innovation, China has gained unique technological advantages in HSR construction. In recent years, China has built a number of HSR lines adapting to special climate conditions, including alpine, high temperature, drought and sandstorm, as well as challenging geological conditions, including soft soil, loess, seasonally frozen soil and Karst areas. As a result, China has gained the capacity to build HSR lines under various geological and climatic conditions.

Thanks to the most comprehensive design and construction technologies and modern equipment, China has built a number of world-class HSR bridges with super long spans, such as Nanjing Dashengguan Yangtze River Bridge, Wuhan Tianxingzhou Yangtze River Bridge, Shanghai—Suzhou—Nantong Yangtze River Bridge, Pingtan Strait Bridge for Road and Railway, Wufengshan Yangtze River Bridge and Beipan River Railway Bridge.

China has resolved technical difficulties in building tunnels in urban area with big diameter TBM and in building tunnels with squeezed surrounding rock and built more than 100 tunnels that are over 10,000m long respectively, such as Shiziyang Estuary Tunnel on Guangzhou—Shenzhen— Hong Kong HSR line, Qinling Tunnel Cluster on Xi'an—Chengdu HSR line and New Badaling Tunnel on Beijing—Zhangjiakou HSR line.

China has developed critical track devices, such as high-speed rail, big size turnout, rail fastening, and rail expansion joint, and also built the largest and most advanced ballastless track system in the world, almost 52,700km long main line in total.

▼ 新八达岭隧道
New Badaling Tunnel

▼ 无砟轨道
Ballastless Track

中国掌握了铁路大型客站设计建造技术，创新了规划设计、空间结构、功能布局、流线组织等，实现了铁路与民航、地铁、市内道路的综合布局及各种交通运输方式之间的无缝换乘，有机融合了建筑风格与地域文化，相继建成的北京南站、武汉站、广州南站、上海虹桥站、哈尔滨西站、重庆西站、雄安站、北京丰台站、郑州航空港站、杭州西站等一大批现代化综合客运枢纽，成为铁路形象的新地标、城市发展的新引擎。

中国建立了完整的铁路建筑信息模型（BIM）标准体系，采用BIM技术进行设计、建设和管理，首次形成高速铁路的"数字孪生"。京张高铁、京雄城际在智能化建造、一体化运维、全生命周期管理方面取得重要突破。

China has mastered the know-how to design and construct large railway passenger stations and found new ways in planning and designing stations, determining spatial structure and functional layout of the station and arranging passenger flow at the station. In planning, China has combined railway, civil aviation, subway and urban road in one layout, realizing a seamless transfer from

railway to other modes of transportation. In designing, China has integrated the architectural styles of railway stations with the local culture. A large number of modern integrated passenger transport hubs, such as Beijingnan Railway Station, Wuhan Railway Station, Guangzhounan Railway Station, Shanghai Hongqiao Railway Station, Harbinxi Railway Station, Chongqingxi Railway Station, Xiong'an Railway Station, Beijing Fengtai Railway Station, Zhengzhou Air Harbour Railway Station and Hangzhouxi Railway Station, have been built one after another, becoming new landmarks for the railways and new growth engines for local cities.

China has developed the complete system of railway building information modeling (BIM) standards. BIM technology has been used in designing, constructing and managing railway, forming the first "digital twin" for HSR. Important breakthroughs, such as intelligent building, integrated operation and maintenance as well as life cycle management, have been made in building Beijing—Zhangjiakou HSR line and Beijing—Xiong'an intercity railway.

◀ ▽ 北京朝阳站
Beijing Chaoyang Railway Station

◀ ▽ 郑州航空港站夜景
The Night View of Zhengzhou Air Harbour Railway Station

◁▽ 呼和浩特东站
Hohhotdong Railway Station

南宁东站
Nanningdong Railway Station

△ ▷ 杭州西站
Hangzhouxi Railway Station

▽ 重庆西站航拍图
Aerial Photos of Chongqingxi Station

▼ 北京丰台站
Beijing Fengtai Railway Station

■ 高速动车组技术

中国先后自主设计研制了先锋号、中华之星等动车组，进行了大量运行试验。通过对世界先进动车组制造技术引进消化吸收再创新，批量生产投入运营了和谐型系列动车组。

为适应高铁运营环境和条件，满足更为复杂多样、长距离、长时间、连续高速运行等需求，中国研制了具有完全自主知识产权的中国标准动车组，并批量投入生产运营。2017年6月25日，中国标准动车组正式命名为复兴号。复兴号动车组在安全、经济、舒适、节能环保等性能上有大幅提升，表现出世界一流的卓越品质。列车设计寿命提高到30年，能够适应中国地域广阔、环境复杂的运行条件，满足长距离、高强度运行的需求；采用全新低阻力流线型头形和车体平顺化设计，列车阻力减少7.5%至12.3%，能够有效降低能耗；列车容量增大，旅客乘坐空间更加宽敞；列车设置智能化感知系统，建立强大的安全监测系统，全车部署2500余项监测点，实现全方位实时监测。

根据市场需求和旅客乘坐体验，中国研制了不同速度等级、适应不同运营场景和环境条件的复兴号系列化动车组。

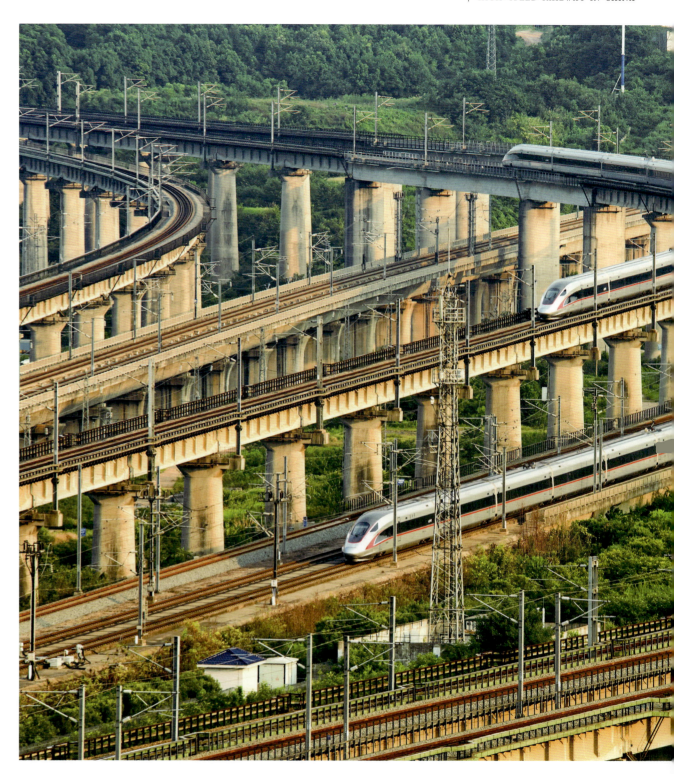

High-Speed Train

China independently developed "Pioneer" and "Star of China" successively and put them into trial run for many tests. On the basis of introducing advanced high-speed train manufacturing technology from other countries and managing to master the know-how, China manufactured a portfolio of Hexie (Harmony) high-speed trains in great batch and put them into operation.

To adapt to the operating environment and conditions of HSR and meet the demands of operating under complex and various scenarios for long distance and long-term at high speed continuously, China has independently developed Chinese standard high-speed train and put it into operation. All intellectual property rights of it are owned by China. On June 25, 2017, Chinese standard high-speed train was dubbed as Fuxing. Fuxing high-speed train shows worldclass performance in its substantially improved safety, cost-effectiveness, comfort, energy conservation and environment-friendliness. With a prolonged life span of 30 years, Fuxing high-speed train can operate for long distance at high frequency in China's vast territory under complex environment conditions. The new streamlined head and smoothened body of the train can reduce the resistance by 7.5% to 12.3%, leading to a effective decline in energy consumption. The train also has a larger capacity and can offer more space for passenger. Equipped with the intelligent sensing system and powerful safety monitoring system, Fuxing high-speed train can make a real-time monitoring over itself with more than 2,500 sensors.

According to demands from market and passengers, China has continued its technological innovation and developed a portfolio of Fuxing high-speed trains, adapting to different speeds, operating scenarios and environment conditions.

◀ 高速动车组在线路上飞驰
The High-Speed Trains Gallop on Lines

研制的时速 350 公里复兴号动车组,在京沪、京广、京张、京津、成渝等高铁常态化按时速 350 公里高标运营,树立了世界高铁运营新标杆。研制的 17 辆超长编组时速 350 公里复兴号动车组,客座席位较标准的 16 辆长编组增加了 7.5%,进一步提升了运输能力。研制的时速 350 公里复兴号智能动车组,在复兴号动车组基础上,优化提升了列车状态感知、故障诊断、安全监控、旅客服务等方面的智能化水平。

China has developed 350km/h Fuxing high-speed train, put it into operation on many HSR lines, such as Beijing—Shanghai, Beijing—Guangzhou, Beijing— Zhangjiakou, Beijing—Tianjin and Chengdu—Chongqing, and operated it at a speed of 350km/h as normal operation, setting a new benchmark for HSR operation in the world. China has developed the 350km/h extra-long Fuxing high-speed train, consisting of 17 carriages. Compared with 16-carriage-train, this train provides 7.5% more seats, increasing the transport capacity of HSR line. China has also developed the 350km/h Fuxing intelligent high-speed train. Compared with the original Fuxing train, this train has improved its intelligent performance in condition sensing, failure diagnosing, safety monitoring and passenger serving.

▲ 时速 350 公里复兴号动车组
350km/h Fuxing High-Speed Train

研制的时速 250 公里复兴号动车组，能耗低、性价比高，可适用于不同运营环境的线路，车体外观涂装以海空蓝和孔雀青作为主色调，被旅客昵称为"蓝暖男"。

China has developed 250km/h Fuxing high-speed train. With energy-saving feature and high cost-performance ratio, this train can operate on lines with various operating conditions. The exterior of this train is coated with sky blue and peacock blue, and therefore it is called "Blue Caring Guy" by the passengers.

▲ 时速 250 公里复兴号动车组
250km/h Fuxing High-Speed Train

▲ 京沪高铁北京南至廊坊间行驶的时速 350 公里复兴号动车组
A Fuxing High-Speed Train Runs at a Speed of 350km/h on Section Between Beijingnan and Langfang on Beijing—Shanghai HSR Line

△ 时速160公里动力集中动车组
160km/h Power Poncentrated Train

研制的时速160公里动力集中复兴号动车组，适用于所有普速电气化铁路，被旅客昵称为"绿巨人"。以此为基础，研制的时速160公里复兴号高原内电双源动车组，两端分别挂有电力动力车和内燃动力车，可在电气化和非电气化线路间自由切换、贯通运用。结合老挝自然环境、线路条件和本土文化，量身打造的时速160公里"澜沧号"动车组，在中老铁路开通时投入运营。

China has developed the 160km/h power-concentrated train, which can run on all kinds of conventional lines and is called "Hulk" by the passengers. On the basis of this train, the 160km/h Fuxing dual-powered train was developed for plateau railway. This train can be powered by electricity and diesel. Electrical motor carriage and diesel motor carriage are arranged at two ends of the train and thus this train can run on both electrified railway and non-electrified railway freely and continously. Considering the natural environment, line conditions and local culture in Laos, China has manufactured 160km/h Lancang train specially for Laos and put it into service when China—laos Railway was open to traffic.

中国按照"集中检修、属地运用、分散存车"的运维布局原则，科学设置了7个动车组高级修检修基地、71个动车运用所、45个存车场等运维基础设施，形成了多元协同、高效集约、覆盖全面、分布均衡的动车组运维布局，满足不同区域、不同车型、不同级别的检修需求。按照"以走行公里为主、时间周期为辅"的原则构建了动车组1~5级修程修制。

Following the principle of "concentrated inspection, local operation and scattered parking", China has rationally set up 7 senior inspection and repair bases, 71 operation points and 45 parking yards for high-speed trains, forming a coordinated, efficient, concentrated, comprehensive and balanced-distributed high-speed train maintenance network. This network can offer inspection and repair service for different high-speed trains from different regions at different levels. According to principle of "traveling distance first and then traveling period", China has established a maintenance regime consisting of 5 levels for high-speed trains.

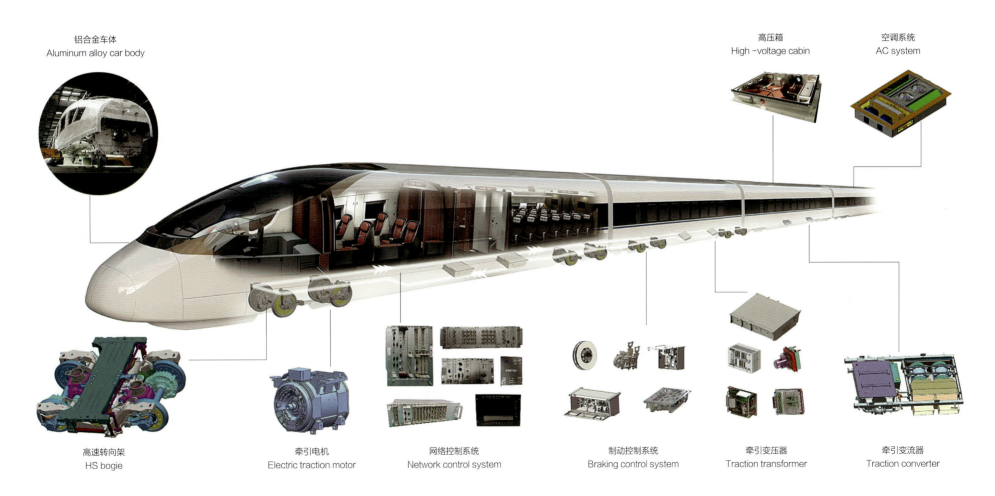

铝合金车体
Aluminum alloy car body

高压箱
High-voltage cabin

空调系统
AC system

高速转向架
HS bogie

牵引电机
Electric traction motor

网络控制系统
Network control system

制动控制系统
Braking control system

牵引变压器
Traction transformer

牵引变流器
Traction converter

▲ 复兴号动车组是由我国自主研发、具有完全知识产权的新一代高速列车。
Fuxing high-speed train are the new generation ones independently developed by China, who owns their complete intellectual property rights.

■ 列车运行控制技术

列车运行控制系统被称为高铁的"大脑和中枢神经",是保障行车安全和列车正点运行的关键系统,结构复杂、技术难度大。经过多年的研究和运用,中国已掌握了高速列车运行控制系统核心技术,开发了具有自主知识产权的列控系统全套装备,达到世界先进水平。

中国制定并发布了符合国情、路情的中国铁路列车运行控制系统(CTCS)技术总体框架,成功研发并投入运用适用于时速200公里至250公里线路的CTCS-2级列控系统、适用于时速250公里至350公里线路的国产化和自主化CTCS-3级列控系统。

中国成功研发并投入使用的高铁自动驾驶系统(ATO),可以根据列车运行计划,结合线路条件和列车性能,为动车组生成最佳的行车速度曲线,能够实现动车组车站自动发车、区间自动运行、到站自动停车、停准后自动开门、与站台门联动控制等功能。

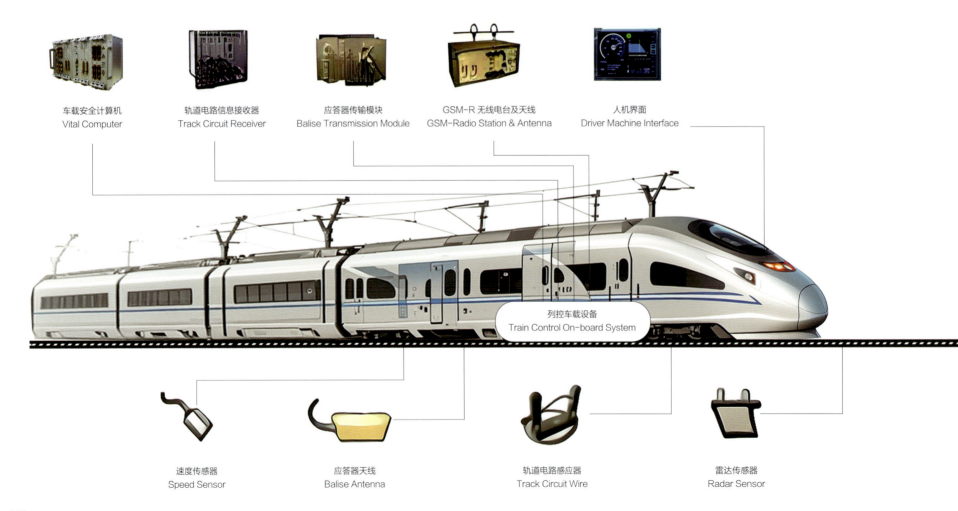

车载安全计算机 Vital Computer
轨道电路信息接收器 Track Circuit Receiver
应答器传输模块 Balise Transmission Module
GSM-R 无线电台及天线 GSM-Radio Station & Antenna
人机界面 Driver Machine Interface
列控车载设备 Train Control On-board System
速度传感器 Speed Sensor
应答器天线 Balise Antenna
轨道电路感应器 Track Circuit Wire
雷达传感器 Radar Sensor

■ Train Control

The train control system, known as the "brain and central nervous system" of the HSR, is a major system ensuring safety and punctual operation of trains. With a complex structure, it is a challenge in technology. After years of research and practice, China has mastered the core technology of HSR train control system and developed a whole set of world-leading train control equipment. All intellectual property rights of the equipment are owned by China.

China has launched the general framework of chinese train control system (CTCS) adapting to conditions in China and its railways and developed CTCS-2 adapting to 200~250km/h lines and Chinese made CTCS-3 adapting to 250~350km/h lines, which have been put into service.

China has developed automatic train operation (ATO) system for HSR. This system can generate the best operation speed curve for the high-speed train according to operation schedule, line conditions and high-speed train performance. With ATO, the high-speed train can automatically depart, operate within section, stop at scheduled stations, open doors after full stop and interact with platform screens.

▲ 中国列车运行控制系统
Chinese Train Control System (CTCS)

■ 牵引供电技术

牵引供电系统是高速列车的动力之源。为适应高铁长距离、高速度、高密度、重负荷的技术要求，通过工程实践和自主创新，中国在高速接触网设计、弓网受流、系统调试等核心技术上实现重大突破，建成了世界上规模最大、布局最复杂的高铁供电调度控制系统，为高铁网提供强大的电力供应保障。

中国成功研制了高铁接触导线及与之配套的接触网部件，构建了满足动车组高速运行条件下双弓受流要求的大张力接触网系统和能够适应动车组长大编组、重联运行、3分钟追踪、时速350公里安全可靠运行的牵引供电系统，建成了世界上规模最大的高铁牵引供电数据采集与监视控制系统（SCADA），建立了中国标准接触网技术装备体系（CRCS），实现了高铁接触网运行状态的动态监测及故障预警，高铁牵引供电整体技术达到世界领先水平。

■ Traction Power Supply

Traction power supply system provides the power to drive the high-speed trains. Meeting the requirements of operating HSR for long distance at high speed and frequency under heavy load, China has made significant breakthroughs in core technologies, such as high-speed overhead contact system (OCS) design, current collection by pantograph from OCS, and system commissioning, after engineering practice and independent innovation. Now China has built the largest and most complex HSR power supply control system in the world and thus ensures a safe power supply for HSR network.

China has developed high-strength contact wire and other matching parts, built a high-tension OCS, from which double-pantograph of high-speed train running at a high speed can collect current, and a safe and reliable traction power supply system, which enables high-speed trains in coupled or extra-long formation to run under 3-minutes headway at a speed of 350km/h. In addition, China has also built the world's largest supervisory control and data acquisition (SCADA) system for HSR traction power supply and China standard OCS technology and equipment system (CRCS), making the dynamic monitoring and failure warning for OCS a reality. All these show that China is world-leading in traction power supply.

▶ 高铁接触网
Overhead Contact System to Power HSR

▼ 接触网相当于火线，钢轨是零线，两者构成一个电回路。钢轨有电流通过，与大地等电位。
The overhead contact line is like a live line and the rail is like a zero line. The two jointly form a circuit loop. The current passes by the rail, while for the current is equipotential to that of the ground.

▼ 受电弓是电力牵引列车从接触网取得电能的电气设备，安装在动车车顶上。
Pantograph an apparatus mounted on the roof of an electric train to collect power through contact with an overhead line.

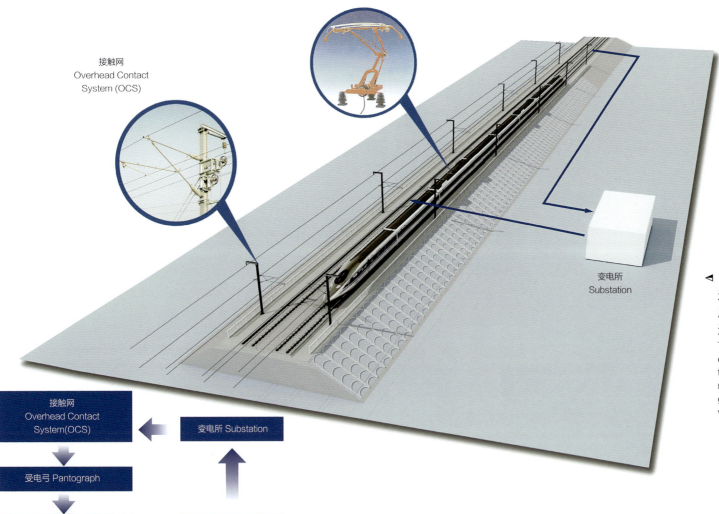

接触网 Overhead Contact System (OCS)

受电弓 Pantograph

变电所 Substation

◁ 变电所将电力输送到接触网上，电力通过动车的受电弓、主断路器引入动车主变压器，然后通过接地线流到车轮上，最后通过钢轨回流到变电所。
The power is first fed by the substation to the overhead contact line and flows to the main transformer of train via the pantograph and main circuit breaker, then to the wheel via the grounding wire and backflows to the substation via the rail.

接触网 Overhead Contact System(OCS) → 受电弓 Pantograph → 动车组 EMUs → 钢轨 Rail → 变电所 Substation → 接触网

中国自主研制的智能牵引供电系统装备在京张高铁正式投入运行,具备健康诊断、故障隔离、重构自愈、运行自律等功能,以及经济高效的特点,成为智能牵引供电系统的标志性工程。

China has developed intelligent traction power supply system and put it into service on Beijing—Zhangjiakou HSR line. This system can diagnose conditions, isolate failures, reconstruct and heal itself as well as run autonomously in an efficient and economical way. Thanks to it, Beijing—Zhangjiakou HSR line has become a landmark project of intelligent traction power supply.

◀ 智能牵引变电所控制室
Intelligent Traction Substation Control Room

■ 运营管理技术

中国拥有世界上规模最大的高铁网，构建了中国国家铁路集团有限公司、各铁路局集团有限公司和车站的三级高铁调度指挥体系，掌握了复杂路网条件下高铁列车运行计划编制和动车组运用综合调度技术，解决了不同动车组编组、不同速度、不同距离、跨线运行等运输组织难题，实现了列车运行设计最小追踪间隔3分钟至5分钟，最大列车密度达到每日160余对。

中国研发了高铁智能调度集中系统，能够实现行车运行调整计划的智能辅助调整、进路和命令的安全卡控；攻克了12306互联网售票系统高并发海量交易、双中心双活等技术难题，系统处理能力和用户体验大幅提升；建设了覆盖"人员—列车—设备—环境—作业"的智能客站，为精准服务旅客、高效组织生产提供了技术支持。

中国建立了完备的高铁技术规章体系，为实现高铁运营安全、效率和效益的协调统一提供了保障。

■ Operational Management

With the world's largest HSR network, China has established a three-level HSR traffic control system, consisting of China State Railway Group Co., Ltd. (CHINA RAILWAY), regional railway group companies and stations. China has mastered the integrated dispatching technologies to develop train running diagram and allocate high-speed

trains in service on such a complex network, and thus managing to dispatch high-speed trains which operate in different formations at different speeds for different distances or cross between lines of different speed levels. The designed minimum headway for trains can be 3~5 minutes. At peak density, more than 160 pairs of high-speed trains are dispatched from two ends of an HSR line a day.

China has developed an intelligent centralized traffic control system, which can realize intelligence-assisted adjustment on train operation plan and control the route and command. China has also resolved the challenges of simultaneously erupting mass trades and dual active-active data centers of on-line ticketing system (www.12306.cn), increased its handling capacity greatly, and improved the experience of users. In addition, China has built intelligent stations that manage information of staff, train, equipment, environment and work, providing targeted customer service and efficient work arrangement.

China has developed a system of operating regulations and rules for HSR, providing technical support for a safe, efficient and economical HSR operation.

Traffic Control Center

◁ 复兴号高速综合检测车
Fuxing Comprehensive High-Speed Inspection Train

■ 风险防控技术

中国构建了闭环管理的高铁安全保障体系，成功研制了高速综合检测列车、高速综合巡检车、工务综合巡检系统，研发应用了供电监测检测系统（6C）、车辆系统（5T），能够实现对设施设备的全方位监测检测；基于车载和地面诊断数据，研发了动车组故障预测与健康管理（PHM）系统，有效提升了动车组远程监控、预警监测、视情维修、健康管理等运维管理水平；采用综合视频监控系统、异物侵限监测系统，实现对列车运行环境的实时监控；研发了自然灾害监测系统、地震预警监测系统，实现对风、雨、雪、地震等自然灾害的实时监测。铁路防灾减灾技术水平持续提升，全方位保障高铁运输安全。

■ Risk Prevention and Control

China has established a closed-loop HSR safety management system, developed the high-speed comprehensive inspection train, high-speed comprehensive patrol inspection vehicle and engineering comprehensive patrol system, and put into operation power supply monitoring and inspecting system (6C) and car monitoring system (5T), which together can monitor and inspect all aspects of HSR equipment. On the basis of on-board and ground diagnosing data, China has developed prognostics and health management system (PHM) for high-speed train, improving the operation and management of remote monitoring, early warning and monitoring, condition-based maintenance and health management. Comprehensive video monitoring system and foreign object intrusion warning system have been used to monitor train operating conditions in real-time. Natural disaster monitoring system and earthquake monitoring and warning system have been developed to monitor wind, rain, snow, earthquake and any other natural disaster in real-time. With all these, China keeps improving itself in preventing and reducing disasters in railways, ensuring transport safety for HSR in all respects.

中 国 高 铁　　HIGH-SPEED RAILWAY IN CHINA

　　经过多年的建设和运营管理实践,中国高铁安全可靠、运力强大、平稳舒适、方便快捷、节能环保、适用性强等特点日益凸显。

After years of construction, operation and management, China's HSR system has been featured as safe and reliable, sufficient and strong, smooth and comfortable, fast and convenient, energy-saving and environment friendly, as well as applicable and flexible.

CHAPTER 第 4 章 中国高铁主要特点

Main Features

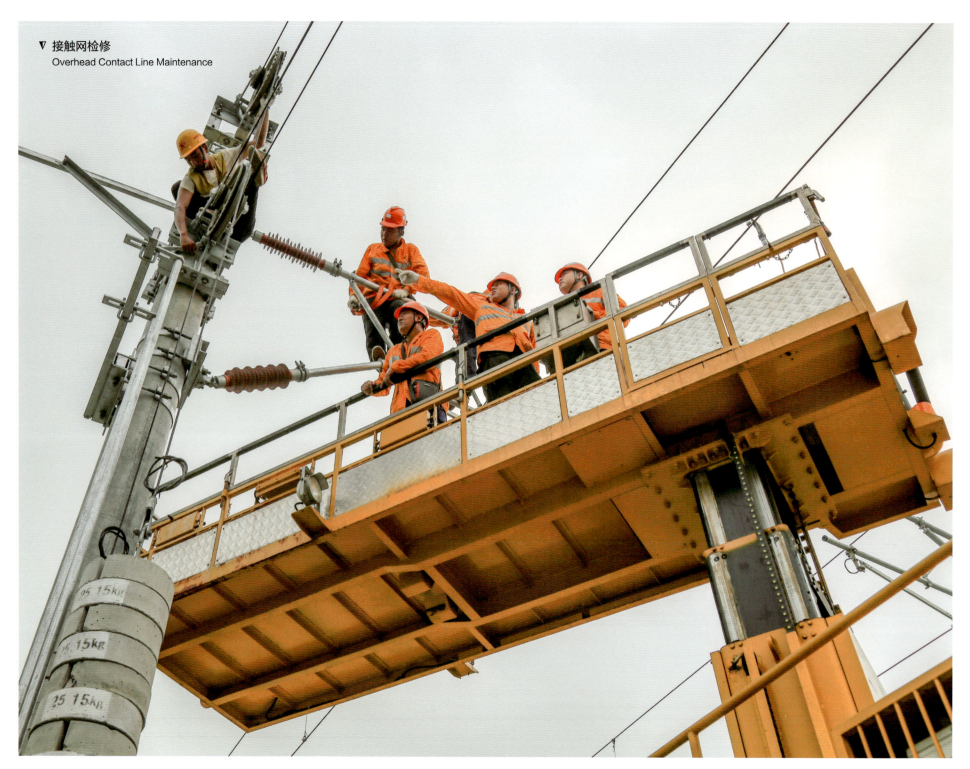

▽ 接触网检修
Overhead Contact Line Maintenance

安全可靠

中国建设了稳固耐久的路基、桥梁、隧道等高铁线路基础设施，制造了安全可靠的高速列车，建立了性能可靠的牵引供电、通信信号等高铁控制系统。经过多年的运营实践，形成了基础设施、移动装备、综合检测、防灾减灾、应急救援为一体的安全风险管理体系，确保高速列车的安全运行。

中国高铁实行全线封闭管理，具有先进的自然灾害及异物侵限监测系统和完善的灾害预防措施、应急救援措施，能够及时发现和处理大风、降雨、冰雪、地震等自然灾害和突发事件。

Safe and Reliable

China has built a solid and durable HSR infrastructure consisting of sub-grades, bridges and tunnels, manufactured safe and reliable high-speed trains, and developed reliable HSR control systems, including traction power supply, communications and signaling. After years of operation, China has established an integrated safety and risk management system over infrastructure, moving equipment, comprehensive inspection, disaster prevention and reduction as well as emergency rescue, ensuring the safe operation of high-speed trains.

China's HSR is fully-fenced and equipped with advanced monitoring system on natural disasters and foreign objects. The complete prevention and rescue measures are put in place against disasters. As a result, natural disasters and emergencies, such as heavy wind, rain, ice, snow and earthquakes, can be timely identified and handled.

▲ 机械师检修动车组车钩
Mechanics Inspect and Repair Couplers of High-Speed Trains

■ 运力强大

目前，中国高铁日均开行动车组列车 7700 余列，发送旅客 790 余万人次。其中，最高峰日开行动车组列车 9500 余列，发送旅客超过 1300 万人次。在节假日和春运等旅客集中出行时期，通过两列动车组重联运行、增开"夜间高铁"等方式，进一步增加高铁运输能力。2023 年 7 月至 8 月的暑期运输期间，全国铁路日均开行动车组列车 8250 多列，发送旅客 980 余万人次，分别占旅客列车开行、发送旅客总数的 81%、76%。

■ Sufficient and Strong

China's HSR a day can operate more than 7,700 high-speed trains on average, handling more than 7.9 million passenger trips. In the peak day, it can run more than 9,500 trains and handle more than 13 million passenger trips. During the traffic rush of festival and holiday, such as the Spring Festival travel rush, two high-speed trains are coupled as one to run and night-time high-speed trains are added to further increase the transport capacity. During the summer travel rush from July to August in 2023, more than 8,250 high-speed trains a day run across China to handle more 9.8 million passenger trips on average, accounting for 81% of trains and 76% of passenger trips handled by railways a day in China on average.

▶ 整装待发
High-Speed Trains Ready to Run

■ 平稳舒适

中国自主创新的钢轨、无缝线路、无砟轨道和高速道岔等技术，保证了高铁线路的高平顺性，使动车组运行更加平稳安全。

中国高速动车组采用了减振性能良好的高速转向架，车厢内振动小。车内采用舒适的软座椅，车窗大、采光好、视野开阔。全自动恒温空调系统能够为旅客提供适宜的车内环境温度、湿度和清新空气。动车组车厢内设有轮椅存放区、婴儿护理桌、无障碍卫生间等，可以满足不同旅客的需要。停车后，动车组的地板与站台可以良好对接，代步工具能够无障碍上下车，为旅客提供了平稳舒适的旅行环境。

▽ 美好旅行生活
Nice Travel Time

■ Smooth and Comfortable

China has independently developed new technologies of rail, seamless track, ballastless track and high-speed turnouts, ensuring the smoothness of HSR lines and the comfort and safety of high-speed train.

China's high-speed trains are equipped with excellent vibration-reducing high-speed bogies, little vibration can be felt inside the train. Cushioned seats and wide windows are provided, bringing comfort, adequate natural light and a broad view for passengers, who can also enjoy moderate temperature and humidity and fresh air provided by a full-automatic constant temperature air conditioning system. Wheelchair storage area, baby-sitting tables and accessible restrooms can also be found inside the carriage, fulfilling different needs of passengers. After door opens, train floor can be well connected to the station platform so that all kinds of conveyances can easily move onto and off the high-speed trains without any trouble. All these together offers a smooth and comfortable travel for passengers.

方便快捷

中国积极推进"高铁网＋互联网"双网融合，建成世界上规模最大的实时票务交易系统，日均售票超过1500万张，单日最高售票2211万张，互联网售票量占总售票量比例高达85%。电子客票基本实现全覆盖，旅客无须取票，持购票时使用的有效身份证件即可进站乘车；计次票、定期票等新型票制产品，可满足商务、通勤等旅客群体出行需求；网上候补购票、在线选座选铺功能，进一步改善了旅客购票体验。

中国高铁客站部署了人脸识别、智能导航等先进的旅客自助服务系统，方便旅客进出站、候车和换乘。采用人性化无障碍设计，设有无障碍售票窗口等残障人士专用服务设施，普遍设置爱心服务区，为重点旅客提供温馨服务。按照"零距离"换乘理念，通过精心合理的场、站布局，使高铁客站与城市公共交通系统甚至机场融为一体，方便旅客在站内顺畅换乘地铁、公共汽车等多种交通工具。

▲ 服务商务座旅客
Business-Class Service

▶ 刷二代身份证进出站
Passengers Tap Their Own Second Generation I.D.Cards to Enter or Exit the Railway Station

■ Fast and Convenient

China has worked hard to integrate HSR network with the Internet and built the largest real-time ticketing system in the world. With this system, more than 15,000,000 tickets on average a day can be sold and a record of selling 22,110,000 tickets in a single day has been made. Now more than 85% of tickets are sold on line. Electronic tickets (e-tickets) are available for almost all HSR lines. Passengers with e-tickets can enter stations and get on the trains just with the effective IDs they use to buy the tickets. There is no need to get printed tickets. New type tickets like multi-ride tickets and periodical tickets are rolled out to meet demands from business people and commuters. Waitlist and seat / sleeper selecting functions on line offer a better experience for passengers.

▲ 北京南站"零距离"换乘示意图
Zero-Distance Transfer Diagram in Beijingnan Railway Station

CHINA RAILWAY has equipped HSR stations with advanced self-service systems such as facial recognition and smart navigation to make it easier for passengers to enter or exit stations, wait for trains or transfer to connections. In addition to user-friendly and accessible designs, special facilities such as accessible ticketing service windows for the disabled can be found at the stations. Service areas are set up at all stations to serve passengers in need. Guided by the concept of zero-distance transfer, China has considered well the layout of stations, yards and depots in planning and building modern passenger transport hubs and transfer centers, which integrate railway stations with urban public transport systems, or even airports. As a result, passengers can easily transfer to subway, bus and other public transport at the stations.

▲ 铁路 12306 售票系统
12306 China Railway Online Ticketing System

▶ 电子客票应用
E-Ticket in Use

中国高铁充分保障老年人及脱网人群的出行服务，持续优化人工售票、电话订票等现金购票方式，能够在售票时自动识别60岁及以上老年旅客并优先安排卧席下铺，所有高铁客站保留实名验证和进出站检票人工通道，可为老年人重点旅客提供预约、专区候车、专人引导等便利服务。

CHINA RAILWAY has worked well to ensure the quality service for the seniors and people who cannot access to Internet. With better service offered, they can buy tickets from station ticketing windows or by telephone and pay for the tickets with cash. The ticketing system can automatically identify people at age of above 60 and reserve the lower sleeper for them first. Railway staff is available at all HSR stations to help passengers verify their identity and check their tickets at entries and exits of stations, and provide service including appointment, special waiting zone and escorting to the senior passengers.

▲ 服务老年旅客和脱网人群
Warm Service for Senior Passengers and Off-Line People

中国不断提升高铁的服务品质，高铁客站和列车正逐步实现 Wi-Fi 信号全覆盖，创新推出了线上自助订餐、无线充电、静音车厢、共享汽车、便民托运等服务。

China has kept improving its service in HSR. Wi-Fi is becoming available at all HSR stations and on high-speed trains. New service including self-online food ordering, wireless charging, quiet-carriage, car-sharing ordering and luggage consignment are available for passengers.

▲ 静音车厢服务
Quiet-Carriage Service

▲ 互联网订餐送至车厢
Food Ordered Online and Service

▲ 列车员整理行李
Luggage Is Put in Order by a Train Attendant

▲ 高铁 + 共享汽车
High-Speed Railway & Car Sharing Service

■ 节能环保

合理选线保护生态环境。在线路设计时,充分利用既有交通廊道,减少对城市的分割和土地占用;高铁线路尽量绕避沿线自然保护区、风景名胜区、水源保护区等,保护生态环境。采用埋深800米至1000米、累计长度达110公里的隧道群方式穿越秦岭山脉的西成高铁,最大限度保护了大熊猫、羚牛、金丝猴等野生动物栖息环境。

以桥代路节约土地资源。在有条件、可实施地段采用了占地少的架桥修建高速铁路的方案,与6米填高的路基相比,每公里桥梁可节约土地约55亩(3.67公顷)。

■ Energy-Saving and Environment-Friendly

HSR route is selected rationally to protect ecological environment. When designing the line, the existing transport corridors are fully used, thus not to divide cities or occupy more land. In addition, HSR line is designed to keep away from natural reserves, places of interest and water sources to protect ecology. A tunnel group with a burial depth of 800~1,000m and a total length of 110km, has been built to help Xi'an—Chengdu HSR line run through Qinling Mountains, thus protecting the habitats of pandas, takins, golden monkeys and other wildlife.

During construction, bridges are used instead of sub-grades to save land resources. Less land-occupying bridges are built in appropriate sections. Compared with 6-meter-high sub-grade, each kilometer of bridge saves about 55 mu (3.67 hectares) of land.

▼ 动车组穿过西成高铁秦岭隧道群
High-Speed Train Passes Through the Qinling Tunnel Cluster of Xi'an-Chengdu HSR Line

京广高铁北京西至涿州东区间
Section Beijingxi—Zhuozhoudong of Beijing—Guangzhou HSR Line

科技创新实现节能环保。高铁采用电力牵引，消除了油烟、粉尘和其他废气对环境的影响。高铁客站大量采用节能技术，其墙体、屋顶选用节能新型材料，照明充分利用自然光并采用高效节能灯及智能控制新技术。高速动车组均采用密闭式集便装置，既方便旅客，又保护环境。

Scientific innovation contributes to energy saving and environment protection. Electric power traction is used in HSR, generating no oil fumes, dust or other waste gases to the environment. A lot of energy saving technologies are adopted in HSR stations. New type energysaving materials are used for walls and roofs. As for lighting in stations, natural lighting is fully used together with energy-efficient lamps and new intelligent control technologies. Sealed waste-collecting devices are installed on high-speed trains to collect sewage from toilets and store them in waste containers, bringing about convenience for passengers as well as protecting the environment.

▼ 上海虹桥站屋顶太阳能装备
Solar Panels on the Roof of Shanghai Hongqiao Railway Station

▲ 京雄城际通过村庄时的全封闭声屏障
Full-Enclosed Noise Barrier on Beijing—Xiong'an Intercity Railway

适用性强

中国研制了能够适应高寒、高原、热带等各种复杂气候和环境的动车组列车，覆盖时速160公里、200公里至250公里和300公里至350公里不同速度等级，设有一等、二等、商务等车厢和适宜长途旅行的卧铺动车组；有满足不同运输需求的8辆、16辆和17辆三种固定编组，其中两列8辆编组动车组可重联运行。

Applicable and Flexible

China has developed high-speed trains adapting to various complex climates and environments, operating at three different speed grades of 160km/h, 200~250km/h and 300~350km/h. They offer first-class, second-class and business-class seats or even sleepers for passengers for a long journey. There are three formations of high-speed trains in China to meet different transport needs: 8-carriage, 16-carriage and 17-carriage. Two 8-carriage trains can be coupled together in operation.

▼ 复兴号智能动车组一等座车厢
First-Class Seats of Fuxing Intelligent High-Speed Train

▲ 复兴号智能动车组商务车厢
A Carriage with Business-Class Seats of Fuxing Intelligent High-Speed Train

▲ 卧铺动车组
Sleeper of High-Speed Train

▲ 二等座
Second-Class Seats

▶ 餐吧车
Dining Carriage

中 国 高 铁   HIGH-SPEED RAILWAY IN CHINA

中国高铁网已将中国东部、中部、西部和东北四大板块连片成网，有力促进了区域互联互通和经济社会协调发展。中国高铁正在改变中国人的出行方式，越来越受到人们的青睐，为人民群众创造了美好生活新时空。

China's HSR has linked the eastern region, the central region, the western region and the northeast of China to one network and greatly boosted the regional connectivity and coordinated socio-economic development. China's HSR is changing the way its people travel and getting favored by more and more travelers, thus creating a new era and space for a better life of the people.

第 5 章 中国高铁创造美好生活

HSR for Better Life

■ 极大便利人们出行

有了高铁,中国春运压力得到极大缓解,乡愁不再遥远,回家之路更加顺畅;有了高铁,人们的出行更加便捷高效,旅行时间普遍比过去压缩一半以上;有了高铁,"千里江陵一日还"成为现实,"难于上青天"的蜀道如今不再难;有了高铁,人民群众的出行意愿更加强劲,说走就走、想去就去的旅行唾手可得。"坐着高铁看中国"已成为广大旅客享受美好旅行生活的真实写照,极大增强了人民群众交通出行的获得感、幸福感和安全感。

▼ 旅客在天津站乘车
Passengers Get on Train at Tianjin Railway Station

▲ 坐着高铁看中国
Take a HSR Ride and Explore China

■ Facilitating Travel

The HSR system has greatly eased the pressure of travel rush during Chinese Spring Festival, making people's hometown not so far away and their way home easier and smoother. It has generally reduced the travel time by more than a half, making people's trips more convenient and efficient. Thanks to HSR, "even to Jiangling a thousand li (500km) away, I can make it in a day" has become a reality, and to access Sichuan, which used to be "harder than to access the sky", has become no longer difficult. People are more willing to travel because of HSR and they can take a spur-of-the-moment trip at any time they wish. "Take a HSR ride and explore China" has become the vivid portrayal of passengers who enjoy nice travel time. HSR has significantly increased Chinese people's sense of fulfillment, happiness and security.

■ 带来"同城效应"

高铁极大拉近了时空距离,加强了沿线城市间人流、信息流、资金流的交流,有利于资源整合和优势互补,带来了"同城效应",加快了城市群发展,形成了多个以高铁为线串起的经济走廊。目前,高铁沿线城市一体化发展、协同发展、融合发展已经成为趋势。高铁也改变了不少年轻人的工作方式,催生了高铁通勤族。

▼ 高铁极大促进沿线城市化建设
High-Speed Railway Has Greatly Promoted the Urbanization Along the Line

Bringing about Urban Cohesion Effect

HSR has greatly shortened the distances both in time and space, intensifying exchanges of people flow, information flow and capital flow between cities along the lines, which is good for cities to integrate resources and take advantage of each other's strength. As a result, HSR has brought about an "urban cohesion effect", accelerating the development of urban agglomerations and promoting the formation of many economy corridors connected by HSR lines. Now cities along the HSR lines are tending to develop in a coordinated and integrated way. HSR has also changed the ways of working for young people, producing commuters by fast trains.

■ 催生"高铁+旅游"新业态

高铁扩大了旅游范围,过去许多交通不便的旅游景点,现在可以轻松抵达;过去许多"藏在深闺人未识"的旅游资源,现在得以开发。高铁压缩了在途时间,提升了旅游效率,"快旅慢游"成为现实。高铁带来客流量的增长,陕西佛坪、湖北恩施、安徽绩溪、广西三江、吉林长白山、云南西双版纳、湖北神农架等多地在高铁开通后旅游客流出现"井喷式"增长。高铁连接起沿线旅游资源,形成了高铁旅游经济带。杭州至黄山高速铁路(杭黄高铁)串起沿线西湖、千岛湖、黄山等风景名胜,形成了世界级黄金旅游线。高铁催生了水下摄影师、渔夫模特等新职业,带火了"农家乐"和特色农产品销售,带旺了旅游经济。"高铁+旅游"已经成为旅游发展新业态和人们生活的新方式。

▼▲ 坐着高铁去旅游
Travel by High-Speed Train

■ Cultivating New Tourism

HSR has extended the reach of tourists, who can easily visit scenic spots that used to be hidden due to traffic limits. With HSR, many tourist resources that are far away in the "sealed oasis", unknown to the outside, now have been developed. With less time spent on travel, tourists can spend more time on sightseeing instead. An expectation of "fast travel and slow tour" has become a reality. There has been a "growth spurt" in tourist flows in many places, such as Foping in Shaanxi, Enshi in Hubei, Jixi in Anhui, Sanjiang in Guangxi, Changbai Mountain in Jilin, Xishuangbanna in Yunnan and Shennongjia in Hubei. HSR lines have linked the tourism resources along them and boosted the formation of HSR tourism economic belt. Hangzhou—Huangshan HSR Line connects many popular scenic spots such as West Lake, Qiandao Lake and Mount Huang, forming a world class "Golden Tourism Line". HSR has also contributed to generate new professions such as underwater photographer and fisherman model and made the agritainment get popular and local signature farm produce hot-selling products, boosting the tourism economy. "HSR+Tour" has become the new form of tourism and also a new way of life.

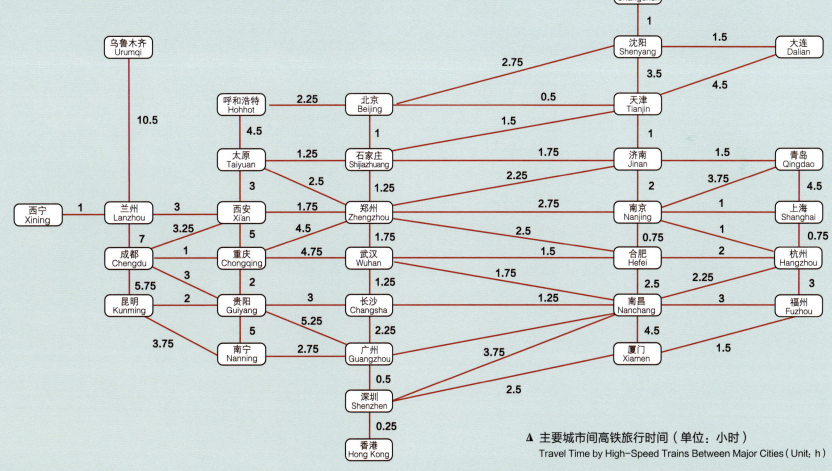

▲ 主要城市间高铁旅行时间（单位：小时）
Travel Time by High-Speed Trains Between Major Cities (Unit: h)

■ 助力区域协调发展

高铁加快了东、中、西部以及东北地区相互间的交流，推动了区域经济社会协调发展，特别是中西部地区一批高铁项目的建成运营，加强了脱贫地区与外界的联系，为乡村振兴提供了加速度、注入了新动能。银西高铁的开通，使陕甘宁革命老区告别封闭，步入经济社会发展的快车道；郑渝高铁的全线贯通，形成西南地区直通中部地区的客运大通道，沿线经济社会发展气象一新；京哈高铁、津秦高铁等项目的建成，大大加强了关内关外的交流。

■ **Contributing to Coordinated Development Across Regions**

HSR has promoted the exchange among the eastern region, the central region, the western region and the northeast of China and boosted the coordinated economic and social development across regions. A number of HSR projects have been put into operation in the central and western regions of China, strengthening the links between the areas just shaken out of poverty and the rest of the China and giving a fresh impetus to rural revitalization. The opening of Yinchuan—Xi'an HSR line to traffic makes the old revolutionary base of Shaanxi, Gansu and Ningxia accessible to the outside world and brought it to a fast track of development in economy and society. The opening of the whole Zhengzhou—Chongqing HSR line to traffic promotes the formation of a big passenger corridor connecting the southwest region of China to the central region of China, bringing about great changes in economic and social development for areas along the line. The opening of Beijing—Harbin HSR line and Tianjin—Qinhuangdao HSR line to traffic greatly boosts the exchange between the northeast China and the rest of China.

▽ 西成高铁
Xi'an—Chengdu HSR Line

◀ 正在飞驰的广深港高铁动感号列车
Vibrant Express Galloping on Guangzhou—Shenzhen—Hong Kong HSR Line

提供繁荣发展新动能

四通八达的高铁网以更快的速度赋能人流、物流、资金流、信息流等生产要素，人们的联系更加紧密了，社会的运行效率更高了，产生了高铁"乘数效应"。高铁改变了中国经济版图，改变了人们的思想观念和生活方式，给中国经济社会发展提供了新动能。

高铁节约社会时间成本，带来了巨大效益。高铁的开通释放了既有铁路线的运能，有力促进了货物运输。高铁的建设和运营，带动了冶金、机械、建筑、橡胶、电力、信息、精密仪器等产业的快速发展，在推动产业结构优化升级方面发挥了重要作用。据测算，我国高铁每1亿元投资，可拉动建筑、冶金、制造等上下游关联产业产值在10亿元以上，创造就业岗位600多个。

Providing a New Growth Driver

With a higher speed, the HSR network extending in all directions has empowered all factors of production such as the flow of labor, goods, capital and information, made people more closely connected, brought about a higher operating efficiency for the whole society, and thus produced the HSR "multiplier effect". The HSR has transformed the territory of China's economy, changed people's views, values, and way of life, and provided a new growth driver for Chinese economy and society.

The HSR system has saved social cost and time cost and brought great benefits. The opening of HSR lines has helped unleash the capacity of the existing lines to transport more freight. The construction and operation of HSR have boosted the rapid growth of metallurgy, machinery, construction, rubber, power, information and precision instruments and other industries and played an important role in upgrading the industrial structure. It is calculated that every 100 million yuan investment in HSR will promote related industries like construction, metallurgy, manufacture to generate output value of more than 1 billion yuan and create more than 600 jobs.

中国高铁　HIGH-SPEED RAILWAY IN CHINA

　　面向未来,中国铁路将深入贯彻落实交通强国发展战略,进一步推进高铁发展,建设更加发达完善的高铁网,推动高铁向更高速、更智能、更绿色方向发展,率先实现铁路现代化,勇当服务和支撑中国式现代化建设的"火车头"。

Looking ahead, CHINA RAILWAY will fully implement the development strategy of building China into a country with great transport strength, further boost the growth of HSR, and build a more developed and complete HSR network. In the future, China's HSR will be faster, more intelligent and greener. CHINA RAILWAY will first achieve the railway modernization and take the initiative to play a leading role as "locomotive" to provide service and support for China on its path to modernization.

第 6 章 中国高铁发展愿景

Future Visions

■ 更完善

进一步提升高铁网的覆盖面和通达性，计划到2035年，高铁营业里程达7万公里左右，50万人口以上城市全部实现高铁通达。

■ **Wider**

China will further improve the coverage and reach of the HSR network. It is planned that the HSR will stretch to a total length of 70,000km in 2035, covering all cities with populations above 500,000 in China.

■ 更高速

实施"CR450 科技创新工程",积极推进基础理论创新和关键技术攻关,研发更高速、更安全、更环保、更节能、更智能的新一代高速动车组,实现更高速度商业运营。

■ Faster

China will implement "CR450 scientific and technological innovation project", promote the innovation in basic theory and tackle key technological issues, and develop safer, more environmental-friendly, energy-saving and intelligent new generation high-speed trains, which will hit a higher speed in commercial operation.

▲ 在福厦高铁湄洲湾跨海大桥,装载 CR450 新技术部件的试验列车以单列时速 453 公里、相对交会时速 891 公里运行。
A high-speed train, equipped with new parts under CR450 program, runs at a speed of 453km/h and at a relative speed of 891km/h when meeting another train at Meizhou Bay Cross-Sea Bridge on Fuzhou—Xiamen HSR Line.

▼ "CR450 科技创新工程"新技术部件试验
Test for New Parts Under CR450 scientific and technological innovation project

▼ 高速机车车辆及动车组整车实验室
Preparation Laboratory for Rolling Stock and High-Speed EMU Test

▼ 最高时速500公里高速铁路轮轨关系实验室
Wheel-Rail Relation Laboratory of 500km/h HSR

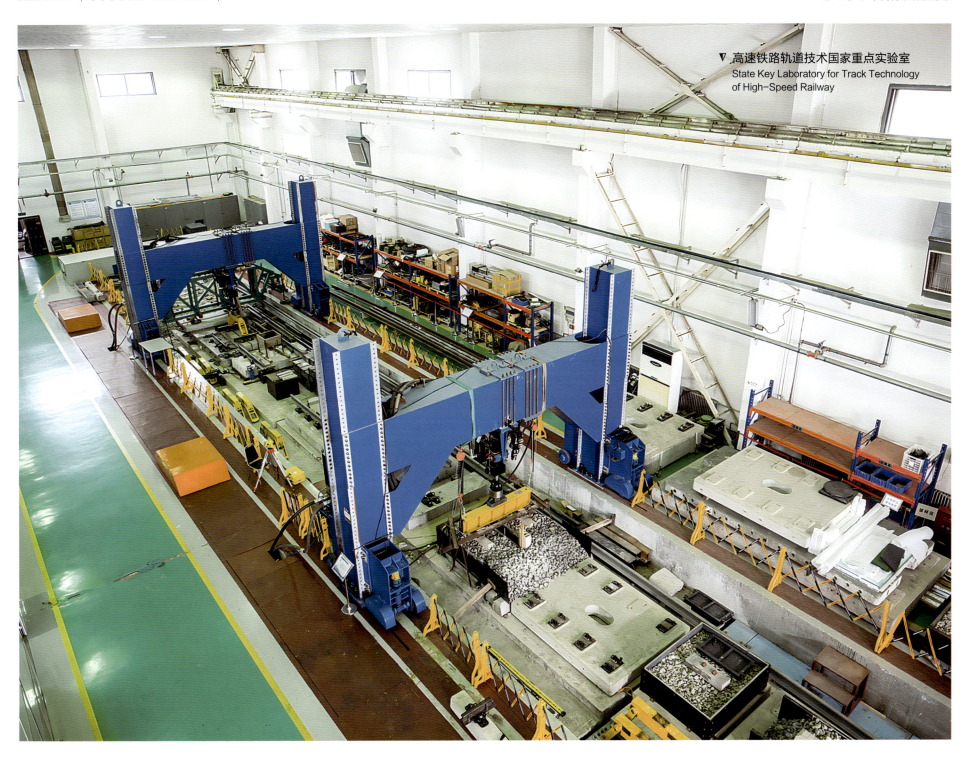

▼ 高速铁路轨道技术国家重点实验室
State Key Laboratory for Track Technology of High-Speed Railway

▼ 国家铁道试验中心环行线
Circular Line of State Railway Test Center

▲ 新型复兴号智能动车组
New Generation Fuxing Intelligent High-Speed Train

■ 更智能

全力推进智能高铁技术创新，广泛应用现代先进技术，实现高铁移动装备、固定基础设施、运营管理及内外部环境信息的全面感知、泛在互联、融合处理、主动学习和科学决策，高铁将更加方便快捷、更加温馨舒适、更加安全可靠、更加节能环保、更加经济高效。

■ Smarter

China will devote great energy to propel HSR technological innovation, apply modern advanced technologies and realize the total awareness, ubiquitous connections, fusion processing, active learning and rational decision making for information of mobile equipment, fixed infrastructure, operation and management, and interior and exterior environments of HSR. With these, China's HSR will be much improved in terms of speed, safety, comfort, convenience, reliability, eco-efficiency, energy consumption and environmental protection.

◂ 新型复兴号智能动车组
New Generation Fuxing Intelligent High-Speed Train

▼ 复兴号飞驰在广西秀丽山川
A Fuxing High-Speed Train Speeds by the Picturesque Mountains and Beautiful Rivers of Guangxi

更绿色

以高铁建设和运营为重点，广泛应用清洁低碳、集约高效、生态友好的先进绿色技术，努力建设与自然资源承载力相匹配、与铁路沿线生态环境相协调的绿色高铁。

Greener

Focusing on the construction and operation of HSR, China will widely adopt advanced green, clean and low-carbon technologies that are intensive, efficient and eco-friendly. A greener HSR system, appropriate for natural resources and the ecological environment along the lines, will be built.

中国高铁　HIGH-SPEED RAILWAY IN CHINA

　　中国铁路积极加强国际合作，坚持高标准、可持续、惠民生，服务高质量共建"一带一路"，与世界共享中国高铁发展成果。

CHINA RAILWAY actively strengthens its international cooperation, pursues high-standard and sustainable development that benefits the people, serves the highquality Belt and Road cooperation, and shares the rewards of China's HSR with the world.

CHAPTER 第 7 章 中国高铁走向世界

Going Global

　　中国与印尼合作建设的雅万高铁，连接印尼首都雅加达和旅游名城万隆，全长 142.3 公里，设计时速 350 公里，2023 年 10 月 17 日开通运营，是共建"一带一路"倡议与印尼"全球海洋支点"战略对接和中印尼两国务实合作的标志性项目，全线采用中国技术、中国标准。开通运营后，雅加达到万隆的旅行时间大幅缩短，可为印尼人民提供高品质出行服务，促进"雅万经济走廊"建设。

Jakarta-Bandung HSR, a cooperation project between China and Indonesia, connects Jakarta, the capital of Indonesia, with Bandung, the famous tourist city. On October 17, 2023, this 142.3km HSR line, with a design speed of 350km/h, was put into operation. It is a landmark project under the synergy of China's Belt and Road Initiative and Indonesia's Global Maritime Fulcrum, and also a result of the practical cooperation between China and Indonesia. The whole line is built using China's engineering technology and standards. When Jakarta—Bandung HSR opens, it will shorten the travel time between Jakarta and Bandung greatly, serve Indonesian people with quality travel, and boost the development of "Economic Corridor along Jakarta—Bandung HSR".

◀ 雅万高铁综合检测车
Comprehensive High-Speed Inspection Train for Jakarta—Bandung HSR

▽ 雅万高铁德卡鲁尔车站
Tegalluar Railway Station on Jakarta—Bandung HSR Line

▼ 动车组行驶在雅万高铁帕达拉朗至卡拉旺区间
A High-Speed Train Runs on Section Between Padalarang and Karawang on Jakarta—Bandung HSR Line

匈塞铁路是中国与中东欧国家合作的旗舰项目，连接塞尔维亚首都贝尔格莱德和匈牙利首都布达佩斯，是中国铁路技术装备与欧盟铁路互联互通技术规范对接的首个项目，全长341.7公里，塞尔维亚段设计时速200公里，匈牙利段设计时速160公里。匈塞铁路塞尔维亚境内贝尔格莱德至诺维萨德段于2022年3月19日开通运营，给沿线民众带来全新出行体验。

Budapest—Belgrade Railway, a flagship project of the cooperation between China and Central and Eastern European countries, connects Budapest, the capital of Hungary, with Belgrade, the capital of Serbia, in total length of 341.7km, with design speed of 160km/h in Hungary and 200km/h in Serbia. It is the first project of applying Chinese railway technology and equipment according to Technical Specification for Interoperability of European Union. Section Belgrade—Novi Sad in Serbia of Belgrade—Budapest Railway was opened to traffic on March 19, 2022, bringing about fresh travel experience for people along the line.

◂ 旅客乘匈塞铁路列车愉快出行
Passengers Enjoys the Travel on Budapest—Belgrade Railway

▲ 首趟列车自贝尔格莱德站始发
The First Train Departed from Belgrade Railway Station

面向未来，中国铁路秉持构建人类命运共同体理念，愿与世界各国共享中国高速铁路发展经验，为各国人民美好旅行生活贡献中国智慧和中国方案。

Facing the future, CHINA RAILWAY will uphold the philosophy of building a community with a shared future for mankind, share its HSR development experience with other countries in the world, and contribute China's wisdom and solutions to better travel and happy life of people across the world.

中国高铁 | HIGH-SPEED RAILWAY IN CHINA

▲ 列车奔驰在匈塞铁路
A Train Runs on Budapest—Belgrade Railway

后　　记

为展示奋力加快建设交通强国，努力当好中国式现代化开路先锋的成就，让国内外更好地了解中国交通发展，我们策划出版了"中国交通名片丛书"，其中《中国高铁》分册由中国国家铁路集团有限公司组织编写。

本书编写力求科学严谨、求真务实，参与本书编写的有：罗传宝、何峰林、武新星、张兆程、郭福成、杜铮、邹朝辉。为本书提供照片的有：史家民、原瑞伦、杨宝森、罗春晓、杨建光、陈涛、翟现亭、王明柱、唐振江、蒋志飞、段倬、闫波、王玮、何坚强、伍光钦、丁波、彭琦、赵萌、虞明、杨林、刘慎库、徐刚等。谭小建对全书进行了统稿。宋强太主持本书编写工作。李军亮对本书内容进行了翻译。

人民交通出版社和中国铁道出版社对本书的出版非常重视，人民交通出版社领导舒驰、刘韬、陈志敏，中国铁道出版社领导王滨、岳震、杨新阳多次提出宝贵意见。赵静、曾亚非、刘莎、曲乐、刘彩云、高鸿剑等同志为本书编辑做了大量工作。

同时，我们要特别感谢所有为中国高铁事业默默奉献的科技工作者、建设者和管理者，是他们的辛勤付出与不懈努力，铸就了今天中国高铁的辉煌成就。我们希望《中国高铁》，能够全面展现中国高铁的辉煌成就，分享中国高铁的发展经验，传递中国高铁背后的故事与精神。

受编写资料和篇幅所限，本书难免挂一漏万，存在不足之处，欢迎广大读者提出宝贵意见、建议，便于我们及时修订完善，以期更好地宣传好、展示好这张"中国名片"！

编者
2024 年 9 月

EPILOGUE

In order to show the achievements of building China into a country with great transport strength and being the trailblazer in China's modernization drive, and enable domestic and international readers to better understand China's transport development, we have planned and published the "Card Book Series: Transport in China", of which the volume titled "High-Speed Railway in China" is organized and compiled by China State Railway Group Co., Ltd..

When compiling this book, we strive to be scientifically rigorous, realistic and pragmatic. This book is edited and compiled by Luo Chuanbao, He Fenglin, Wu Xinxing, Zhang Zhaocheng, Guo Fucheng, Du Zheng, and Zou Zhaohui. The photos used in this book are provided by Shi Jiamin, Yuan Ruilun, Yang Baosen, Luo Chunxiao, Yang Jianguang, Chen Tao, Zhai Xianting, Wang Mingzhu, Tang Zhenjiang, Jiang Zhifei, Duan Zhuo, Yan Bo, Wang Wei, He Jianqiang, Wu Guangqin, Ding Bo, Peng Qi, Zhao Meng, Yu Ming, Yang Lin, Liu Shenku and Xu Gang. Tan Xiaojian does the final compilation and editing and Song Qiangtai takes charge of the whole compilation of the book. Li Junliang translates the content of this book.

China Communications Press and China Railway Publishing House attach great importance to the publication of this book. The management from China Communications Press, Shu Chi, Liu Tao, and Chen Zhimin, as well as the management from China Railway Publishing House, Wang bin, Yue zhen, and Yang Xinyang, have provided valuable suggestions on multiple occasions. Zhao Jing, Zeng Yafei, Liu Sha, Qu Le, Liu Caiyun, and Gao Hongjian have done a great deal of work in editing this book.

At the same time, we would like to express our special gratitude to all the scientific and technological workers, builders, and managers, who have silently contributed to the cause of China's high-speed railway. It is their hard work and unremitting efforts that have led to the brilliant achievements of China's high-speed railway today. We hope that this book can comprehensively display the remarkable achievements and share the development experience of China's high-speed railway, and convey the stories and spirit behind it.

Due to the limitation of compilation materials and space, there are inevitably many deficiencies in this book. We welcome readers to put forward valuable opinions and suggestions so that we can revise and improve it in time and better display this "business card of China".

Editors
September 2024

图书在版编目（CIP）数据

中国高铁：汉文、英文 / 中国国家铁路集团有限公司著 . —北京：人民交通出版社股份有限公司：中国铁道出版社有限公司, 2024. 9. —ISBN 978-7-114-19684-3

Ⅰ. U238

中国国家版本馆 CIP 数据核字第 2024LC3422 号

审图号：GS 京（2024）1928 号

本书由人民交通出版社与中国铁道出版社有限公司联合出版发行。未经著作权人书面许可，本书图片及文字任何部分，不得以任何方式和手段进行复制、转载或刊登。版权所有，侵权必究。

Copyright © 2024

All rights reserved. No part of this publication may be reproduced, stored in a retrieval system, or transmitted in any form or by any means, electronic, mechanical, photocopying, recording or otherwise, without the prior written permission of the copyright holder. Printed in China.

Zhongguo Gaotie

书　名：	中国高铁
著 作 者：	中国国家铁路集团有限公司
责任编辑：	曲　乐　曾亚非　高鸿剑　刘彩云
责任校对：	赵媛媛
责任印制：	张　凯
出版发行：	人民交通出版社　中国铁道出版社有限公司
地　　址：	（100011）北京市朝阳区安定门外外馆斜街3号
网　　址：	http://www.ccpcl.com.cn
销售电话：	（010）85285857
总 经 销：	人民交通出版社发行部
经　　销：	各地新华书店
印　　刷：	北京雅昌艺术印刷有限公司
开　　本：	965×635　1/8
印　　张：	21.5
字　　数：	218千
版　　次：	2024年9月　第1版
印　　次：	2024年9月　第1次印刷
书　　号：	ISBN 978-7-114-19684-3
定　　价：	368.00元

（有印刷、装订质量问题的图书，由人民交通出版社负责调换）